D1212145

DUE NORTH

DUE NORTH

by

MYRTLE SIMPSON

LONDON
VICTOR GOLLANCZ LTD
1970

First published October 1970
Second impression November 1970

ISBN 0 575 00585 8

Printed in Great Britain by
The Camelot Press Ltd., London and Southampton

The money for this expedition was put up by the *Daily Telegraph*, the *Sunday Telegraph* and the *Daily Telegraph Colour Magazine*, of London. The members of the expedition take this opportunity of thanking the managers of these newspapers for giving them the chance of achieving their objective—the North Pole.

"I want to go to where the lines of latitude do not matter."

ROGER TUFFT

"To strive, to seek, to find and not to yield."
'ULYSSES' BY TENNYSON

Inscribed on the cross erected at Cape Evans in memory of Scott's party who failed to return from the South Pole

CONTENTS

LIST OF ILLUSTRATIONS

DUE NORTH

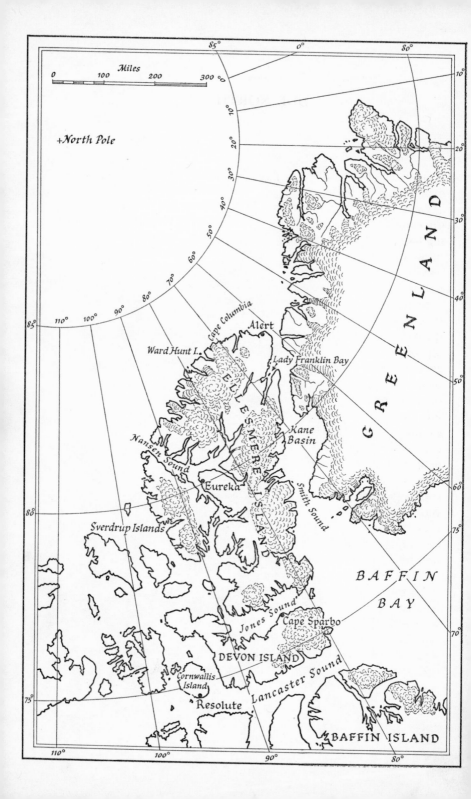

CHAPTER ONE

I GAZED DREAMILY out of a chink in the frost on the little oval window of the rattley plane. The noise was a thankful barrier between me and the four other occupants of the limited space unoccupied by skis, boxes and tent. The outlook into the gloaming had not changed for four hours. The vista was of flat acres of snow, ridges of mountains and ripples of darker white petrified waves on the polar sea. Now and then I scraped with my fingernail to keep my spy-hole free.

Suddenly I was jolted into life as the arched backs of the mountains surged up towards my eyes. My ears screamed—and the de Havilland Otter landed effortlessly on a little lake on the top of the Canadian map. I felt elated, as if our journey was over, forgetting that it had not begun. Breathless with excitement I pushed past Hugh and Roger and scrambled out through the door. I jumped down into the twilight. The air was soft and absolutely calm. So this is what it felt like, I thought, gazing about. The tip of the Americas: Ward Hunt Island, 83 degrees North (83°N). It was incredibly beautiful. Outlines of people and plane were numbed in the gentle light. My feet were silent on the snow. A pink blush covered one arc of the sky, as if dawn would explode into brilliant light at any minute. But I knew this to be delusion, as the sun was not going to rise over that horizon for some time yet. A cone of snow reared up on my left hand forming the bulwark of a mountain. I turned my back to it, sensing satisfaction from its solidity in this ethereal world.

Light cascaded out of the plane and there was an area of feverish activity within its bounds. The pilot, Weldy Phipps, wanted to be off. His stocky frame filled the door repeatedly, masking the light, as he unloaded his plane of our gear. Our white polystyrene boxes glinted as Weldy handed them down into my husband, Hugh's, outstretched arms. He in turn stacked them up beside our friend Roger, who was organising the sledge. Buzzing on the outskirts was the American photographer, Fred, who was bustling about with his cameras, catching his big gauntlet gloves between the many straps entwined about his neck. Away back through layers of fur I could detect a little patch of his white, friendly face. The features of the *Daily Telegraph* reporter were easier to make out; they were pressed against the glass of one window of the plane. He was busy with his notebook, his fingers describing accurately "what it looked like". But, I thought, what is the good of that? He'll never know "how it felt". He would not know that the air had a texture; that the muted sound of one's feet on the snow had to be sensed in order to comprehend the primaeval environment that surrounded us; that one had to stand there, away from the plane, in order to feel the emptiness.

The layers of boxes became higher and higher on the sledge. I wanted to involve myself with the action, so lifted one end of the tent and struggled to place it on top of the load. "Are you taking that grand piano all the way?" shouted Weldy, as he threw out the last pair of skis. He was only too right. The sledge looked unwieldy and far too heavy even to push across the flat lake. For the first time since the conception of our plans, self-confidence faltered.

I was a child when I learnt the lesson that the world is a lonely place. I had found out that it was no use to wait on the off-chance that someone else would come along and lift one over the proverbial stile. One had to struggle entirely by one's self. By my own efforts I had grown up, earned a living, travelled abroad. I had climbed the highest mountain in Peru, all 22,200 feet. I had skied across Greenland, 400 miles of it from east to west. But now, I felt that awful physical sickness that means fear. I did not know if I was big enough for this. My inadequacies, and Hugh's and Roger's for that matter, seethed up in my mind. I felt horrified at the presumption that had made me say with bravado for the past year, "I am going to the North Pole."

"Say, can I do anything for you?" said Fred, the photographer, offering me his hand.

"Yes," I said, tears suddenly welling up in my throat. "Kiss my kids."

"Sure, sure," he answered, gripping my arm, emotion husking his Yankee voice. "I know you'll make it. I'll be there at the Pole to watch you coming in."

The still air was shattered as Weldy swung his propellers into life. "Come on," he roared out of the window, but the American had a second thought. He ran off a few yards, to kick a stone free from the ice. He scooped it into his big palm, then bustled up into the plane. "What's the name of that mountain?" I shouted to Weldy, running up to his window. Suddenly it seemed to matter to me enormously that our area of snow and ice had been identified and actually had a name. "Mount Walker, after a young geologist who died of cancer in his brain. There is a hut over there, you know," he added. "Dates from the '60 U.S.-Canadian polar-shelf project. Probably some fuel left too. Don't use those drums though," pointing to two half-buried in snow. "That's my emergency aero juice." I paid little attention. I was not interested. We had no use for a hut here, and paraffin was our fuel.

Weldy lifted one gauntlet glove in a casual farewell. His plane sat lightly as a fly on the surface of the snow. In a few seconds it was off. It rose into the air and made a bee-line south. I watched, my eyes riveted to the dark smudge in the sky, fading fast into the horizon. Nothing moved. Utter silence. We were completely on our own. "What on earth are we doing here?" I said aloud, unnecessarily, knowing that the answer lay in the magnetic attraction of the North Pole.

The Danes have a word for it, "Polarhuller", and we were far from the first to fall under the spell.

The earliest written account of travel within the Arctic circle is by Pytheas. This navigator and geographer set out from Greece in 325 B.C. with the intention of searching for amber and tin. It was a private venture and he had limited means. He visited Britain and Norway and gave an account of islands he called Thule, six days' voyage to the north. He was a good astronomer and one of the first to fix latitudes and to arrive at a correct notion of the tides and their connection with the moon. The Greeks had already come to the conclusion that north of the Arctic Circle there must be sun at midnight in the summer and none at midday in the winter.

The general view was that the polar regions were uninhabit-able frozen zones, but there was also a less scientific notion that there was a happy region, north of the north wind, where the sun was always shining, and the inhabitants, the Hyperboreans, led a peaceful untroubled life.

The first authentic voyage into Arctic waters was recorded at the court of King Alfred. This voyage was possibly commis-sioned by the King, making it the first sponsored polar expedi-tion. Alfred's captain, Ottar, was after the whale and walrus. The tusks they used for arrowheads, and the hide for the hawsers that hoisted the sails, and the cables that held the anchor, in order to keep the big ships off the rocks.

If the recent Vinland map is authentic, the Vikings knew the Polar sea as well as the Atlantic, and sailed as far north as latitude 83°. They were the first navigators in history who willingly left the coasts and sailed into the open ocean. Their explorations were commercial too, but also in search of new land for settlement. In the years overlapping the sixteenth and seventeenth centuries, the Dutch and English attempted to break the trading monopoly of Spain and Portugal with the Orient, by searching for a new route to the Pacific, sailing north, then turning right to the east and picking a way round the hump of Norway past Bear Island, Spitzbergen and the fabulous islands of the Samoyeds towards Nova Zemlya, fringing the top of Finland and Russia.

Willoughby sailed from Deptford on May 10th 1553. His ships followed the route of the Norsemen and eventually rounded the Kola Peninsula, and sailed thankfully into the tranquil white sea. They were surprised to find the civilised monastery of St Nicholas near the mouth of the Devina river, later to become the site of Archangel. This voyage is very important in British polar history, as it led to the charter of the Muscovy company of Merchant Adventurers, which gave a fresh impetus to arctic discovery when a brisk trade sprang up between England and Russia; between them, ships were financed to sail farther afield. The Muscovy company proved to people in England that there was some useful return from a polar voyage, which meant that money was forthcoming to despatch adventurers to push forward discovery to the west as well as to the east. So Davis, Fox and Frobisher sailed out of England and brought back descriptions of pack ice and also accurate accounts of the strange, outlandish people called "Eskimo".

The best servant of the Muscovy company was Henry Hudson. His first voyage was undertaken in 1607 when he discovered the most northern known point on the east coast of Greenland. On his way home he discovered the island now called Jan Mayen which he named "Hudson's Tutches".

On a second voyage he sailed round the edge of the pack between Spitzbergen and Nova Zemlya, but on a third voyage the ice compelled him to return westwards and unexpectedly he found himself exploring the coasts of North America and discovering the Hudson River. In 1610 he entered Hudson Strait and found the great bay which bears his name. He was forced to winter here, undergoing incredible hardships as he had no clothes or camping equipment for the cold. On his way home his crew mutinied and set him and his little son, with some sick men, adrift in a boat, and the explorer perished in the seas that he had opened up.

William Baffin outdid Hudson's enterprise and in 1615 sailed far up the west coast of Greenland to latitude 77°45′N, the farthest north in that area for 236 years. Interest in the Arctic now declined. The wealthy merchants felt that there were easier ways to make their pile, and they realised that the north-east and north-west passages were too difficult to be commercially worth while.

Expeditions up to now had been made by navy men, ship based, who made no attempt to travel overland unless forced to do so. They had little knowledge of polar currents and conditions, and most ships turned home in late August when ice conditions were at their best for northerly sailing, as they were terrified of wintering hemmed in by ice. The ships were small and they could only move when the wind was in a favourable quarter, which happened seldom. Long sojourns in the ice were impossible for these early men because they were unable to preserve food.

Little happened in the north during the years leading up to the Napoleonic Wars and no further voyages of discovery were made until after the peace of 1815, when North Polar research came into vogue once more. The English government, in fact, made a law by which a reward of £20,000 was offered for making the North-West Passage and £5,000 for reaching 89°N. The British navy was the richest and the largest in the world and the Admiralty sent out various expeditions into the Greenland area. Whaling ships were also out on the Polar Sea and one, captained by William Scorsby, brought back the first description of the "ice blink", showing the presence of ice in open water. Captain Scorsby was also the first to be aware of the ice drift off the east Greenland coast. This information was later developed and successfully used by Nansen in his drift off the Fram. However the first person to show interest in the North Pole itself—as opposed to the purely mercenary concern of finding the North-West Passage—was a British navy admiral.

Parry in 1830, sailed a wooden ship, the *Hecla*, out of England and into the ice north of Spitzbergen. He then set off on foot, his seamen hauling a lifeboat over the frozen ice. He spent thirty-five days on the pack going north, but came to the horrifying conclusion that his party was actually drifting south faster than progressing in the right direction. However, he did reach 82°40'N. before turning back. Scurvy ravaged his men and he only just made his ship. He was bitterly disappointed as he had based his plans of success on Scorsby's description of ice floes "so smooth that a coach might have been driven over them".

The challenge was taken up by others, but no one got very far. The explorers were still navy men, ship orientated, with few clothes for the cold and no lightweight equipment. Their boats were heavy and cumbersome and the men were only really at home on the sea.

Sir John Barrow had founded the Geographical Society in 1830. Coincidently he became Secretary to the Admiralty, and he pointed out to the First Lord that one more attempt should be made to complete the discovery of the route from the Atlantic to the Pacific. There was only a comparatively small gap unexplored between Parry's farthest westerly point, Melville Island, and the Great Fish River on the American continent. Barrow urged the navy to move now and he pointed out that two stout ships, the *Erebus* and the *Terror*, were ready to hand, seasoned and undamaged after a successful four-year Antarctic expedition, under James Ross. "If the completion of the passage be left to be performed by some other power," said Barrow, "England, by her neglect of it, having opened the east and west doors, would be laughed at by all the world for having hesitated to cross the threshold."

So, victualled for three years, the two ships sailed out of Greenhithe on May 19th 1845, equipped with the new fangled "steam power", for emergency use. They were under the command of Sir John Franklin, aged 58, who had three previous voyages to the north to his credit. The men aboard numbered 129, but only three of the twenty-two officers had been to the Arctic before. Franklin was intensely happy during the voyage to Greenland, and wrote glowing accounts to his wife of his growing affection for his men and the excitement as they sailed up the west Greenland coast, and put into Disco Bay during the third week in July. There they were seen on July 26th by a whaler and were at that date moored to an iceberg waiting for a favourable opportunity to enter the ice of Baffin Bay. From that day not one of Franklin's men have been seen alive, apart from vague reports and stories that have drifted south by wandering Eskimos.

The Admiralty had instructed Franklin to cross the Barrow Strait and penetrate west through any convenient channel which might exist through the archipelago until the shores of Cornwallis or Devon Island or even Melville were reached.

The outlines of the adventures of the *Erebus* and *Terror* were eventually filled in thanks to the efforts of Lady Franklin the first woman to have her name coupled to arctic exploration. Jane Franklin was blue eyed, small and slightly built. She was extremely energetic, and kept voluminous diaries and long accounts of her travels and activities. She first met her husband while visiting Captain John Ross's ship, H.M.S. *Isabella*, armed with an introduction given her by Dr Roget, who had taken time off from compiling his *Thesaurus* to write it for her. Lieutenant Franklin was in charge of a small ship, the *Trent*. He had never sailed north before, but had proved himself in the eyes of the Navy by serving at Trafalgar, as a signal midshipman, on the *Bellerophon*. Some historians note that it was likely that young Franklin was the officer that saw, and reported to his captain, Nelson's celebrated message, "England expects every man to do his duty." The *Trent* reached latitude 80°37'N and arrived home leaking and damaged on October 22nd 1818.

Franklin soon married, to an Ann Porden, who was involved in a club to which Jane also belonged. The women saw each other often, and Jane brought presents to the Franklins for the sailor to take on his trips: a silver pencil, a pair of fur gloves, books. Ann was a frail, ailing woman, and died while Franklin was on his second land-expedition north. On his return, Jane was soon writing in her journal, "Captain F. called in evening . . . begging acceptance of reindeer tongues and three pairs of shoes made by native Indian woman." They were engaged the following September and went to Russia together, where they dined with the Empress Mother. Jane was "Mrs" for only five months when she was stepped up to "Lady".

Sir John was offered the Governorship of Tasmania in 1836, and he and Jane set off for the penal settlement with a small retinue in a little ship, the *Fairlie*. A man was lost overboard, and the ship was nearly run down by a whaler off South America, but five months later they sailed into Hobart, and made a public landing between rows of convicts. Jane was the first woman to climb Mount Wellington, and also claimed fame by attempting to rid the island of snakes: she offered one shilling to any convict that produced a head, and was £600 down in the first year!

There was great excitement in Tasmania when the ships *Erebus* and *Terror* called in en route for the Antarctic, under James Ross. Little did Jane realise the significance of this encounter with the ships and their crew.

Franklin was nudging sixty when offered command of the expedition sent officially to tie up the loose strands of the North-West Passage. Jane was delighted, and set to work to make him a flag to take on the voyage. A few days before he was off, Franklin lay down beside his sewing wife. He drifted into sleep, and Jane threw the flag over him as a blanket. This woke up the tired explorer. "Why," he exclaimed, "what have you done? Don't you know they lay the Union Jack over a corpse?"

So Franklin disappeared into the Arctic never to be seen
again. But Lady Franklin was insistent that her husband was
alive, and when an account reached her, in 1854, of an Eskimo
named In-nook-poo-zhee-jook having seen an exhausted,
hungry Englishman struggling on the ice near the mouth of
the Great Fish River, she resolved to send out yet another
expedition to search. There had already been over forty, a
number of them financed by Lady Franklin, and the rest the
result of her appeal to the Admiralty and the colonies for
money. The British Government spent £675,000 on search and
relief expeditions, and the Admiralty offered £20,000 for the
discovery of the ships. The convicts in Tasmania sent £1,700
and various private citizens something like £35,000. By 1854,
Britain was engulfed in the Crimean War, and the government
felt that they could not possibly justify yet another search.

But while reports of casualties in the Light Brigade, due to
their useless charge, flooded London, and headlines told of the
"Lady of the Lamp", sympathy and admiration for Lady
Franklin was such that a ballad appeared at the same time, for
sale in the London streets, called "Lady Franklin's Lament".

> "In Baffin's Bay where the whale fish blows,
> Is the fate of Franklin—no one knows.
> Ten thousand pounds would I freely give,
> To learn that my husband still did live.
> And to bring him back to a land of life
> Where once again I would be his wife. . . ."

Lady Franklin now spent the remains of her private money
to buy a steam yacht, the *Fox*, and fit it out for a long voyage in
a north-westerly direction. An old Arctic hand, M'Clintock,
agreed to captain the ship for free, and she sailed from Aber-
deen on July 1st 1857. M'Clintock had mustered a crew of
twenty-five worthy old shipmates and well tried men, and
himself was an authority on the Eskimo way of life, and how to
live off the land. The *Fox* carried food, for twenty-eight months,
that included preserved vegetables, lemon juice and pickles,
plus, a present from the Admiralty, 682 pounds of pemmican,
to be eaten on every third day. This pemmican was made

of prime beef, cut into thin slices and dried over a wood fire. Then it was pounded up, and mixed with an equal weight of melted beef fat, before being run into strong tin cases with convex ends, thus giving them greater resistance to the claws of polar bears.

One of the thickest ice-years on record was the year 1857, and the *Fox* soon became caught in the pack off Baffin Bay. Held fast she drifted south for the next eight months, but was only slightly damaged in spite of travelling 1,395 miles completely at the mercy of the ice. Finally released into the swelling sea, the *Fox* now nearly met disaster. Huge pieces of ice, tossing, twisting, smashing into each other, converged on the ship from all directions. However, M'Clintock, devoted to Lady Franklin, was prepared to try again instead of scurrying south. He turned the ship's head north once more, and had nursed the *Fox* up to the tip of the Boothia Peninsula by the time the second winter set in. M'Clintock now left the ship and took to the ice, and made various sorties into the surrounding area. Once spring came, he set out in earnest, determined to contact the Eskimos on the westerly coast of the peninsula, and quiz them on the authenticity of the story of white men being seen on the ice.

M'Clintock carried a very small brown-holland tent, mackintosh floor-cloth, and felt robes, and each man had a bag of double blanketing and a pair of fur boots for sleeping in. They carried no spare clothes. At night his party spent two and a half hours building a snow hut, and then carefully stowed away everything that the dogs might eat! This included sledge-harnesses, boots, mitts and even the sextant. The tent was thrown over the hut to form a roof, as M'Clintock said he never had time to perfect the technique of building in snow. His roofs always fell in. The men then crawled inside, blocking the door behind them with snow. The lamp was lit, foot-gear dried, diaries written up, watches wound, sleeping-bags wriggled into, pipes lighted and the merits of the various dogs discussed until supper was ready.

The dogs were badly affected by the cold, and most of them were soon lame from hard particles of snow, like grains of sand. M'Clintock then harnessed up his seamen, and this "man-hauling" method made him the first man to perfect a mode of travel that was independent of a ship or even Eskimo dogs; by this method he subsequently covered 1,300 miles on the sea ice, averaging nineteen miles per day.

As they plodded along, the men talked of the happy Christmas which they had spent on the *Fox*, celebrated with a large cheese, venison and beer, eaten off snow-white deal tables, after which a fresh supply of clay pipes had been handed out to each seaman. Candles had superseded the usual smoky lamps. Outside a fierce nor'-wester howled through the rigging, and drifting snow rustled past. No stars had penetrated through the thick gloom, and the thermometer varied between 76 degrees and 80 degrees below. Now, on the ice, it was minus 48 degrees. On March 1st M'Clintock camped at about the position of the magnetic north pole. He had almost decided to turn back, as no trace of Franklin or Eskimo had been seen, and his party was very nearly out of food. M'Clintock walked away from the camp to look ahead, when suddenly he saw four figures appearing. As they drew nearer M'Clintock's eyes were caught by a glint of metal gleaming on the front of one of the figures' sealskin anorak. A naval brass button!

M'Clintock knew he was on to something at last. The figures were Eskimo and one said he had taken the button from a white man, dead of starvation on an island nearby. The iron for their knives had come from the same place. Next morning an entire village population arrived at M'Clintock's camp, through a howling gale, all delighted to show their treasures: silver spoons and medals, a gold chain, more naval buttons, and plenty of knives and bows and arrows constructed of materials from a ship, forced on shore by ice at a place on King William Island, named Oot-loo-lik.

M'Clintock devoted the rest of the year to following up every clue given to him by the Eskimos. He never saw the wrecks of the *Erebus or Terror*, but came home with conclusive evidence of their fate. His experiences left a larger imprint on polar exploration than merely closing the Franklin saga. His success with manhauling a sledge influenced Scott to adopt the same technique on his journey to the South Pole, and it was his method that we were to use on our expedition 110 years later.

The pattern of British Naval arctic explorers was broken by a

Norwegian—Fridtjof Nansen. Nansen is my hero. His writing of the high Arctic scene set off a yearning in my heart to travel in such places and see them for myself. Like me, Nansen had trudged his home hills alone since his early teens. He felt a need to go into the solitary places, enjoying the feeling of being self-sufficient and looking after himself under all circumstances. This love precipitated him, at the age of twenty-one, into his first Arctic adventure. He joined the crew of a Norwegian sealer and sailed towards the east coast of Greenland. The ship became becalmed, then frozen fast into the ice. For twenty-four days it drifted along the coast in full view of an unknown world. Nansen climbed the maintop many times a day to gaze through his glasses over the fields of floating ice to the peaks and glaciers glittering in the daylight beyond. Nansen was entranced with the wild beauty of the scene, particularly at night when the sun sank lowest, blazing the sky behind the hills. He considered making an attempt to reach the shore over the ice, but the captain vetoed his suggestion. However, Nansen returned in his own ship five years later, to find out what lay beyond the coastal hills.

Amassing his experience gained from living in the Norwegian mountains in winter, he knew just what equipment was essential. He loaded this on to a sledge and, with five companions skied right across Greenland from east to west. On September 24th 1888, they reached the land of the west coast. They could see a river winding through sandy flats into a blue expanse of fjord. Nansen wrote that they "were so excited we ran down, threw our bundles into the heather and ourselves by their side, and allowed the consciousness of having reached our destination to comfort and soothe our wearied bodies". They still had to reach a settlement along the rugged coast. Undaunted, Nansen's companion, Sverdrup built a boat. The hull was the canvas floor of the tent, the sides twigs of dwarf willow, the thwarts the theodolite stand, and two thin pieces of bamboo provided, in Nansen's words, "the scantiest seats it has ever been my ill luck to sit on." The boat leaked, so whenever the weather became stormy they had to put into shore. They lived off gulls as they wended their way slowly along the coast. Nansen wrote that there was no word in the language to describe the satisfaction of the savage who sat and dipped his hands into the billy-can to fish out the body of a gull and thrust it into his hungry mouth. The glow from their fire was dimmed by the glory of the Northern Lights. One day they landed for lunch and found masses of blaeberries. Having had no fresh fruit for months they were delighted.

"First we ate the berries standing, and then when we could stand no longer we ate them sitting, and when this posture became at last too wearisome, we lay prone at our ease and prolonged the debauch to incredible lengths."

They reached Godthaab on October 3rd. Nansen was met with the news that he had passed his doctorate degree!

Nansen went home, but his interest in the Arctic Ocean was rekindled when he read an old newspaper report of the disaster to an American ship, the *Jeanette*. She had foundered on the ice in 1879, off the coast of Siberia. Three years later, a pair of oilskin breeches and some papers were found frozen into the ice at Juleanehaab on the south-west coast of Greenland. There could be only one explanation—the belongings from the *Jeanette* must have drifted in the pack ice right across the Arctic Ocean.

Nansen had a bright idea. There must be a deep channel flowing from Spitzbergen towards Greenland. His theory was backed up by Siberian driftwood having been found in large quantities on the Greenland coast, and the evidence of a Siberian harpoon throwing-stick having ended up on the west coast, near Godthaab.

Nansen explained his theory to the Royal Geographical Society in London: "I believe that if we take careful notice of the forces which nature herself places at our disposal, and endeavour to work with them and not against them, we will find if not the shortest, in all events the most certain route to the Pole." It took Nansen nine years to get his expedition off the ground, but, on June 24th 1893, his ship, the *Fram*, with thirteen men on board, set sail to put his theory to the test. As he left Norway, and the *Fram* sailed down the fjord into the northern Arctic Ocean, Nansen said, "I will never retreat. I will go through to the other side."

He succeeded in getting the *Fram* as far north as 83°59', but this was not far enough for Nansen. So, with two men and three sledges, he set out on foot. Taking food for one hundred days, loaded on three sledges, and pulled by twenty-eight dogs, they struggled north. To start with, it was too cold and Nansen returned to the ship. They set out again and eventually reached 86°13′ latitude. At this point the northerly direction was blocked by a "veritable chaos of ice-blocks", and Nansen decided to turn back, but of course he did not now know the position of the *Fram*. So he decided, matter-of-factly, that the easiest thing to do was to walk to the land instead of looking for the ship. Fifteen months later Nansen stumbled into the very English Jackson-Harmsworth expedition that was geologising on Franz Joseph Land.

Nansen, temporarily separated from his companions, was picking his way along the coast through a tumbled collection of rocks and boulders when suddenly he thought he heard a human voice—a strange one, the first for three years.

"How my heart beat," he wrote, "and the blood rushed to my brain, as I ran up on to a hummock and halloed with all the strength of my lungs. Behind that one human voice in the midst of the icy desert, this one message from life, stood home and she who was waiting there. Soon I heard another shout and saw too, from an ice ridge further in, the dark form of a figure. It was a dog, but farther off came another figure and that was a man."

Nansen approached him; raised his hat; the man did the same.

"How do you do," he said, as he drew near, extending a hand. He wore an English check suit and high rubber water-boots, was well shaved, well groomed, with a whiff of scented soap perceptible to the wild man's sharpened senses.

After a few moments of polite conversation the man said, "Aren't you Nansen?"

"Yes, I am," replied the explorer, clad in dirty rags, black with oil and soot, and with long uncombed hair and shaggy beard. "By jove," was the retort. "I am glad to see you."

He seized Nansen's hand and shook it again, while his whole face became a great smile of welcome, and delight beamed from his dark eyes. The British party engulfed Nansen with friendliness. They took him back to their little hut and he was soon surrounded with the luxuries of good living—water, soap, towels and clean clothes.

"What has happened?" wrote Nansen in his diary that night. "I can scarcely grasp it. How incessant are the vicissitudes in this wandering life. A few days ago swimming in the water for dear life, attacked by walrus, living the savage life which I have lived for more than a year now, and sure of a long journey before us over ice and sea, through unknown regions before we should meet with other human beings. A journey full of the ups and downs, the same disappointments that we have become so accustomed to, and now, living the life of a civilised European! Do I sleep, do I dream, do I wonder and doubt?"

That was the end of Nansen's North Pole venture, and he returned to Norway.

In 1909 a staggering announcement filled the American newspapers. A Doctor Frederick Albert Cook had reached the North Pole! Accompanied by two Eskimo boys, Ah-we-lah and E-tuk-i-shuk, he arrived at the Pole at noon, April 21st 1908. He had then spent a year getting back to civilisation and was still relating his experiences when another American, Robert Peary, denounced Cook and stated that he had just returned from the Pole himself!

Peary had strong backers—Theodore Roosevelt, the Colgates and the National Geographical Society—all very wealthy and influential, and his claim was upheld. With his negro servant, Henson, and four Eskimos, he was credited with having travelled over the pack for thirty-six days, arriving at the Pole on April 7th, 1909. Cook was naïve, a lone wolf and an outsider first and last. He was hounded out of the country and the Explorers' Club of New York hastily dropped him from their rolls. A bitter squabble resulted, with followers of Cook reiterating their beliefs in the likeable, easy-going doctor, and pointing out flaws in Peary's story. Much more doubt has been cast on Peary's claims recently and evidence produced to the effect that he could not possibly have reached the Pole because the speed he claimed was fantastic. It was like stating one had run a mile in two minutes but unfortunately producing no reliable witnesses of the feat. Peary was not very expert in the use of his sextant and made no account, either, for the drift of the ice.

Meanwhile, another Norwegian, young Amundsen, was laying plans for an attempt on the North Pole. Hearing of Peary's success, he switched his venue to the South, sailing off in Nansen's ship, the *Fram*, to beat Scott on that epic journey that culminated in the tragedy of the British party dying one by one eleven miles from their food depot. Amundsen's change of plan resulted in the North Pole being empty and alone for nearly sixty years. Then another Norwegian, Bjorn Staib, tried to travel over the polar pack in 1963, and reached 86°N, when he had to bail out and board an ice island occupied by the Americans. In 1968 Wally Herbert set out to attempt to traverse the Arctic Ocean from Alaska to Spitzbergen, with plans to call in at the North Pole on the way.

Wally and another American, Plaisted (who travelled on ski scooter), and Staib all needed planes. Aircraft had to drop them fresh food, new sledges and tents as the occasion arose, and had also to show them the way. Their mode of travel was dependent on re-supply. None of these expeditions was self-sufficient in the field, and they only carried supplies for a short time.

Our expedition was to be on classical lines and our mode of travel was closer to that of my hero, Nansen. We wanted no planes buzzing overhead to turn the journey into an artificial project. Our intention was to try to go it alone. To be totally self-sufficient and to have enough food and fuel on our sledge, hauled behind us, to last the 470 miles between North Canada and the North Pole. This was the challenge. It so happened that a Canadian party of scientists were to be at the Pole during two weeks of April in 1969, working on gravity measurements. Our plan was to rendezvous with them, and for me to fly out, then Hugh and Roger would ski on to Greenland, completing our journey from the New World back to the Old.

CHAPTER TWO

THE FIRST STEPS of our journey actually took place on January 28th 1969, when I sat in Montreal Airport feeling like a destitute European migrant among the smart, svelte set of people that inhabit the airports across the world. I had bundles of sleeping bags, armfuls of jerseys and loose pieces of luggage, and it was *my* three children, scruffy already, who were attracting attention, noisily skidding over the highly polished floor, trundling our baby Rory in the airport's smart pram. Heads turned as three anoraked and booted figures came towards me looking bizarre in the surroundings. "Plane's cancelled," shouted Hugh. "They are going to put us up at an hotel." My heart sank. We were dressed for stepping out of a plane into a temperature of minus 60 degrees Fahrenheit, and for moving into an Eskimo hut. I had only vast, clumsy, insulated boots to wear, and worse, only four more paper nappies for Rory. The horror on the face of the hotel receptionist would have been even worse if she had realised the hell that was to be the next three days.

The cancelled plane was to have taken us to Resolute, an Eskimo settlement and weather station on Cornwallis Island in the Canadian Northern Territories at 75°N. Here we intended to stay for a few weeks while I established the children in an Eskimo school. Then Hugh, Roger Tufft and I would fly 800 miles farther north to Ward Hunt Island, the tip of the land comprising the Americas. From there we would set out on skis, unsupported by aeroplanes, snow tractors or dogs, for our attempt to cross the pack ice and reach the North Pole.

Our aim was not purely geographical. Hugh is a pathologist and his line of medical research has involved him in the study of human rhythms. The heart beat is a good and obvious example of a rhythmic process but the ones he was particularly interested in were slower, having a cycle of about one day. Usually these keep time by an average twenty-four hour routine which is constantly giving clues of time to the organism. In polar regions the unusual illumination in summer and winter means that the most important of these clues—light and dark— is lost. Hugh wanted to find out what happened to these rhythms under this circumstance; did they wander off twenty-four hours, as happens, for example, to men living down caves without watches? Could the disorganisation of rhythms explain a hysterical disease called pibloctoq to which the Eskimos are prone, since certain brain rhythms might be altered? Indeed, pibloctoq might be a model for schizophrenia, one of the most obscure of medical problems, in that those with the disease have time clues, but their bodies seem to be unable to use them.

The study was to be part of a world wide survey of rhythms, in the International Biological programme. Roger and I and Hugh were to be guinea pigs. Our rhythms were to be studied by collecting a few cubic centimetres from every urine sample which would later be analysed for hormones and salts which have a circadian, or twenty-four-hour, rhythm of excretion. The adrenal hormones, like cortisone, for example, may show a threefold increase in excretion rate at midday, reflecting higher production, higher blood concentration and greater effect on all our tissues.

During a study carried out in the summer light of Spitz-bergen, Hugh had shown that when a man lives on a twenty-one-hour day/night system instead of a twenty-four-hour one, the adrenal rhythm, far from adopting the twenty-one-hour routine or sticking to the twenty-four-hour routine, usually goes slightly slower (24·24). He considered this to be the evolutionary, inherited rhythm into which the organism relapsed whenever presented with an artificial routine cycle too different, or in a place with no time clues at all. In this way the functional activity of the organism becomes impaired, since habit and physical capability may be out of step.

As we would be setting off in the winter, the time of constant darkness—and our journey would last through into late spring when the sun would be perpetually in the sky—Hugh was excited about the potential of the research project and expected much light to be thrown on the subject by our results.

There was a lot of information on the subject of Hugh's

research. But only a handful of people in the world today have had any experience of travelling in the polar pack itself.

The passengers eventually collected again for the plane to the North. Our few companions were easy to identify among the well-heeled airport crowd. Fur hats, fur jackets to the knee and with luggage in rucksacks or bags. A few minutes' flight out of Montreal, and there was nothing below except water and woods. I shifted the weight of Rory on my knee and considered whether he should have been here at all. We were advancing into a world where to survive one must come to terms with the elements. We were leaving behind the tin gods of our generation, the TV sets and the latest cars. "Escapist" I am often called, but I consider it easier to hide among the artificial values of life at home, cosseted by electric blankets and lulled by machines turning the washing and sparkling the plates. There is little room for personal choice in the urban world—one is not even allowed to die in peace. I thought of the boredom of so many suburban wives preoccupied with gossip, their only incentive to be one above the Joneses next door. But was it fair to have our children with us as we flew away from hospitals, their schools, fresh fruit and carpeted floors?

Actually it never occurred to me to leave them behind. "But why take the children?" I was asked a thousand times. My answer was that a family should stay together and therefore I had carried my children through the tropical jungles of Guyana, the glaciers of Greenland (the year following our crossing of the icecap) and the empty beaches of the Caribbean coast. But on this journey the children could only come so far. We would leave them at Resolute to go to the little school, with round-faced almond-eyed Eskimo children; to be taken care of by Sandra Stewart, sitting behind me now in the aeroplane telling my eight-year-old Bruce that he must not ask for another Coke, her loud Scots accent reverberating through the plane.

A newspaper at home had suggested that we needed a baby-sitter for our expedition. Two thousand girls had applied! Sandra stood out among them, bright and enthusiastic; forth-right but competent and kind. I felt that she would cope with the rough white men encountered in the North and equally well with the gentle Eskimo women, those of the deep dark eyes and long silences of their race.

Our other companion was Roger Tufft. He is a Welshman but we had forgiven him that long ago. Hugh had first met him in the Antarctic fifteen years before, and together they had made many, long, sometimes desperate, dog sledge journeys inland. He had come with us to Spitzbergen, an island of glaciers and raw rock, cold and gaunt in the winter, but in the summer a lovely place to be. The plants and mosses start to stir early, ready to burst into flower as soon as the snows have gone. As the sun rises in the sky, this tundra land wakes up and the heat of the sun thaws out the ground to a depth of a few feet. Below, the land remains frozen hard and impenetrable. The fringe of life on the surface is full of colour and lushness, quite unexpected in the so-called "barren lands" of the North. The birds know about these glorious northern wastes and start to arrive as soon as the sun. Roger, Hugh and I had left my baby in the care of our other companions, including Wally Herbert, and had travelled on to the ice cap and climbed a mountain called Anafjellet away to the far north. We reached the summit after a hard ice climb and looked across the Arctic Ocean. There was nothing more of the world. Nothing in between us and the Pole, but 650 miles of snow and frozen sea. My heart stirred, I remembered, with a desire to go and travel to that spot on the earth where the lines of longitude converge.

That experience occurred in 1960. In 1965 Roger had come with us to Greenland, when we had followed Nansen's route and skied four hundred miles from east coast to west right across the inland ice. Roger had been always cheerful, with something new to say, and I knew him to be just the man to come with us now on this adventure.

Hugh had lifted the telephone one evening a year ago in our Glasgow house and dialled the number of Roger's Cumberland home. "That you, Rog? How about the North Pole? Man-hauling. Lightweight."

"All right," said Roger, and I could visualise a broad smile creeping slowly over his face. "I've been thinking about that for some time."

Myrtle Simpson with icicled eyelashes, fringe and frozen nose peers out from the inner world of her anorak hood. On polar pack, March, 1969.

Hugh Simpson on Devon Island, N.W.T. August, 1969.

Roger Tufft.

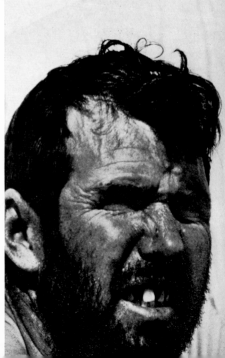

Misty dawn over Arctic Ocean. The fog is due to open water. Myrtle Simpson and Roger Tufft, March, 1969.

Roger was originally to be one of Wally Herbert's team for his traverse of the Arctic Ocean, but had opted out as he considered that the constant dependence on planes made the journey too artificial. Like us, he felt that Wally's plans were becoming top-heavy, and the money involved ridiculous. Wally needed £100,000. We were limited to £10,000.

For hours we flew over the empty land, but the scene had changed now into a dull darkness. These were the barren lands beyond the tree line. The pale sun sank. "Watch it," Roger told nine-year-old Robin. "You won't see it again for some time." More hours passed until there was suddenly activity in the plane. Lights sprang up out of the inky darkness and we put down at Frobisher to refuel. I bundled the children into their anoraks and we stepped out into minus 35 degrees Fahrenheit. The cold caught at my chest but otherwise it was exhilarating. A heavily jacketed man hustled us through the pitch dark into a hut for the hour's stop. I was immediately accosted by a youth with a tape recorder. "CBS News" he announced in a demanding voice, thrusting a microphone at my face. His rudeness infuriated me but I stumbled out answers to his persistent Americanese. "Say," he said, turning to Bruce, "what's it like to have a mother leaving you to go to the Pole?"

"O.K., O.K.," answered Bruce, mimicking already, "but could you tell me where the lavatory is?"

"Oh, you've spoilt my tape," muttered CBS in petulant tones, fiddling with his knobs. "You've wasted ten minutes of my time."

As soon as I re-entered the plane I was conscious of a complete change in atmosphere. It was now crowded, but a relaxed timelessness seemed to emanate, quite unlike the jostle of the West. A girl sat in my seat. She turned her face to me. It was round with beautiful dark almond eyes and inky black, dead straight hair cut in a fringe. She wore a white anorak made of blanket material, or duffel, and out of the folds of the hood, which lay on her shoulders, peeped a minute baby, its sloe eyes gazing at the light. I felt Rory an overgrown elephant as I sat beside her. She lifted her baby out of the amautie, or hood, and Rory fingered its tiny feet, watching the microscopic toes wriggle. When the trim hostess handed out our meal, the

Eskimo girl put her baby back into her hood, leaving two hands free, while I had to struggle with mine on my knee.

Frobisher to Resolute is as far as Frobisher to Montreal. Hours and hours droned by till we bundled out again. Too tired to be excited, I pushed the wooden children down the steps. The cold had a texture that actually bit into one's skin. I thrust Rory down into the bottom of his sleeping bag as I staggered along behind. There was a grey light, like 3 p.m. in December at home in Glasgow.

"Oh, Pudluk," Hugh was saying warmly to an Eskimo, at the bottom of the steps, who had a grin right across his face. Hugh had been here before, on a reconnaissance the previous September. An extraordinary vehicle stood behind Pudluk, a tank track on one side, a wheel on the other. The shape was of a praying mantis. "It's a moon truck," said Robin, echoing my thoughts, as the Eskimo lifted the children into the cab, and Sandra and I squashed in alongside. Hugh and Roger climbed in the back.

Around the airstrip was "The Base". Stationed here were more than one hundred men, mostly Canadians with a smattering from the U.S.A. They were met. observers, radio men, technicians, drivers and workmen and they lived in a centrally heated atmosphere of 75 degrees Fahrenheit in plush prefab huts. Our destination was the Eskimo village of Resolute Bay, four miles away. Pudluk pulled on the levers of his "Bombardier" and the vehicle shuddered into life. We jolted from the base over acres of flat snow and across a scene which was a dull white in the twilight. "Why isn't it day yet?" asked Rona. I explained again that it would not be for several weeks yet. Little buildings took shape ahead and then Pudluk came to a stop under a tall pole from which flapped a huge red and white Canadian flag. "There," he said. "That's Sudlavenik's house. That's for you." He was pointing down below us, a hundred yards down a steep slope, and right beside the line of rough ice which marked the edge of the sea. A dozen or so round bundles had collected from nowhere. They were children, wrapped up in fur, reminding me of young owls, all feathers and in a row. Giggling and jostling each other, they suddenly moved. They threw themselves down on their bums at the top

of the steep slope and slithered at high speed to the foot. I
noticed that Robin was already in their midst. Enchanted, I
jumped out, then clutched the bundle of Rory in his sleeping
bag as Sandra handed him down. I tried to kick steps down the
slope, but there was only one good way, so we resorted to our
beam ends too. By the time Sandra and I reached the house, it
was overflowing with children. The walls of the porch were lined
with ice but the inner room was warm and cosy and immediately I knew that we could make it home.

Rory had sunk deep into his bag, fast asleep. I looked about
for somewhere to put him. A young girl held out her arms. She
wore a maroon anorak, with black fur around her smooth,
calm face. She smiled at the baby like a madonna. We had
lived with hunting Eskimos in Greenland, where everybody's
baby was for loving and women cuddled and fed any child.
They were too kind and warm-hearted to limit their affection
to the close family unit. As I watched this girl now, I felt a
great happiness that the Eskimos of Canada had managed to
retain at least this quality of their own way of life.

"Quick," we heard Hugh yelling down at us. "Get the tinned
food in before it freezes."

I then remembered our mountain of equipment.

There were sixty children in the village and each one enthusiastically joined in the task. Using the boxes of food as tobog-
gans, they shrieked with laughter as they shot down from the
huge pile of stores and equipment that Hugh and Roger had
unloaded from the vehicle. I was soon surrounded by tons of
parcels and boxes as Sandra and I tried to stow it all away in
the house.

I knew that there was little hunting in and around Resolute
now, and we had been told that the organisation of the co-op
shop had collapsed and that it had run out of stores several
months before. So I had brought enough food for Sandra and
the children to last for six months, plus sledging rations for our
journey to the North, camping equipment, clothes, nappies,
pots and pans, school books and reams of paper and crayons, a
spirograph, plasticine, and, for a forgotten reason, a jigsaw of a
racing car.

All the children buzzed about, laughing at Sandra and me

engulfed in luggage as the pile at the top of the slope grew less and the chaos around the house mounted. Suddenly the chattering of the swarm of children was silenced. The activity froze. I looked up from a case of dried milk to see why. A tall, fine, incorruptible looking man stood at the door, a beaver-skin hat in his hand, sealskin kamiks up to his calves, and the letters R.C.M.P. inlaid in fur. It was the Mountie! I breathed a sigh of relief. The children would be safe in a community with a bloke like that around. He eyed my children, Sandra and me, and silently assessed the piles of food that I was stacking against the walls.

"So you're going to the North Pole," he said, in a tone of voice that implied that there were plenty of cases of madness in the North already. He spoke slowly, his Canadian tones soft after the ugly shrill voices from the U.S.A.

The Mounties are not quite the king pins of the North that they used to be, but their enthusiasm for the Eskimo way of life is directly responsible for what is preserved and what substituted for it under the blanket of American culture—jeans, Coca Cola, tin-pot disc-jockey music and the comic strip "book". Our Mountie—Ken Gaab, with weathered face and straight back—looked as if he would do better than that, but the local children gave him a wide berth, their animated faces closing into a deadpan look as they melted into the background.

"Better shift these tins before they freeze," he said, leaning against the door, and I wondered if he would lend a hand. I indignantly felt that he should, as his presence had not only paralysed my Eskimo help, but Sandra too, whose Scottish Nationalist front was suffering from surprise at being impressed by anything furth of the border.

"Look, look," said my children, hovering round a bright blue vehicle of motor-bike size, glinting in the fading twilight outside.

"That's my Ski-doo," said Ken.

"Can I have a ride?" asked Sandra, quick as a flash.

"Not just now," he replied firmly, with a hint of better things to come. "I must be off."

He mounted his smart snow scooter, treating it like a horse. He stood up on it and knelt on one knee on the saddle, holding the handlebars as if reins. He took off with a spurt of snow tossed into the air behind, and the rest of us resumed the work of stowing away our stores. I was dead tired. A billy-can of water hissed on the stove and thankfully I made some tea.

Everyone in the village was as intrigued to see us as we were to see them. Fur-haloed adult faces were glued to the windows, flat noses squashed even more as they pressed against the glass. I asked one of the mass of children inside his name. "Noah 947," he replied. Up till recently the Canadian government had numbered the Eskimos rather than named them. I had lived with the Greenland Eskimos, and their self-respect, enthusiasm and full life is a reflection of the administration by the Danish government, whose attitude has been to foster the continuation of a traditional Eskimo culture while assimilating what is good of the West. In Canada government guidance has been virtually non-existent until very recently. And the policy now is of "cultural replacement" which means the eradication of anything that is "different" in the local way of life.

Hugh and Roger pushed their way through the crowd and flopped down beside me on a box of food. The expedition had begun. Here we were at 76°N, all our equipment and us under one roof. I looked around with a proprietorial air.

The next three weeks were to be devoted to getting organised. There were two sleeping areas in our little house. In a corner of one of these Roger began to assemble our sledge—our most critical piece of equipment. It had travelled from the Lake District as a bundle of sticks. Roger now lashed the runners to the bridges with rawhide, and as it began to take shape it also took over the space. There were no nails in its construction, each joint must move as a yacht, and take the strain so that it would snake over the rough ground to absorb the shock. British Naval expeditions had manhauled, hitching up a gang of matelots, and used narrow-runnered heavy sledges in order to withstand the battering of the pack. Often they had taken the ship's boat instead of the sledge because they always expected to find open water close to the Pole. The traditional Greenland sledges, however, were always small. The Eskimos lacked the basic raw materials, so used bones and skins as they had no large pieces of wood even for runners. As contact with traders increased, the Eskimos were able to obtain timber and tools to work it, and by Peary's day they built bigger and heavier sledges as a result. These were generally broad with vertical runners but they were very, very heavy and needed a large dog team—perhaps twenty dogs—to make them move. This was the kind of sledge that Peary, Cook, Staib, Plaisted and Herbert used. Nansen, as usual, broke free of everyone else and designed his own sledge. The basic difference was that his runners were much broader and so better in soft snow, and it was far lighter, the complete sledge weighing about 28 pounds. It was made of ash, while the runners were of hickory and shaped like skis in order to carry it over deep snow. To hold the sledge together the various joints were lashed, in Eskimo fashion. No nails or pegs were used.

Our sledge was based on Nansen's lines. It had been built for us by Peter Moffat of Cumberland, one of the few carpenters in Britain who still matures his own wood, taking about ten years to see the process through. All the bridges and curves of the runners of our sledge were laminated and thus immensely strong. Like Nansen's our sledge was of ash and it weighed 52 pounds. The whole principle of the sledge was its lightness and flexibility. It broke away from Nansen's sledge in one respect—our runners were not steel shod, but covered in high molecular weight polyethylene. This is a new-fangled material used on down-hill skis. It was supplied for us by Head Skis of America who have done much research on the subject of friction. Every ski firm hopes the racers will win on their product and Heads were confident that this variant of plastic cell was a major breakthrough for the soles of their skis. Down-hill races are won on ·oo1 of a second and so an infinitesimal advantage was worth thousands of dollars in research.

The bright yellow ski runners looked smart as Roger put the jigsaw together. The finished sledge was twelve feet long, just over one and a half feet wide, and was eight inches high.

Hugh organised his test tubes while I sewed last-minute adjustments to our tent. It was tiny, 6 feet by 3 feet and 4 feet high at the ridge. It was made of windproof cotton with a bamboo frame. Though weight conservation was critical, it was essential in temperatures well below zero that the tent had two layers—with only one, the humid air inside would line the walls with a sheet of ice and all the carefully won heat would escape to the outside. The floor of our tent was made of ultra light-weight, expanded polystyrene, in two-inch thick tiles which would insulate us from the ice below.

I sat on the floor of our hut to sew a wider valance all round the tent. The Eskimo women visitors would silently watch. I was always conscious of four eyes, as there was the inevitable baby peeping out from the anorak hood over its mother's shoulder. The women brought their own work—usually patching kamiks, which the children soon wore out sliding down the icy bank from the school beside the Canadian flag. Using both hands to sew minute stitches, the women's jaws would be champing on pieces of seal skin so as to make it gooey and wet, and easy to cut for patching the children's shoes.

Men visitors would cluster round Roger, fingering the sledge, their older memories stirred. Roger told them of his dog sledging experiences with the Greenland Eskimos, hunting walrus and polar bear. He had wintered in Kanak north of Thule and had made many journeys with the Eskimos over their traditional hunting routes. He had even crossed the sound between Greenland and Canada and travelled down the Ellesmere coast with a well known Eskimo hunter called Peter Peary who claimed to be legitimately entitled to his name. Pudluk and Sudlavenik would gaze longingly as Roger bound the ends of rope and finished off his job to put the sledge in ship-shape condition. They would ask him to tell his story once more.

No one sledges from Resolute now. To do so one would need to own a team of dogs—and the Government would not approve. To them, dogs are noisy and fierce, and ski-doos are far more hygienic. Of course they are also far less trouble and easier to feed, provided one can earn money to pay for the fuel.

Our morning's work was interrupted as our children burst through the door, school over. Rona held her reading book—pictures of suburban children standing waiting for a bus under the shade of a green leafy tree. Noah's mother looked at it, completely baffled. Eskimo life and culture are completely ignored in the educational system of the Canadian north.

"Learnt any of the language yet?" I asked my boys. "We are not allowed to speak Eskimo in the school. A boy got into trouble for it today," was the reply. If I were a Canadian Eskimo parent, I thought, I would be furious at this imposition.

We were interrupted by the rumbling of a Bombardier as the vehicle drew up outside. In lounged some men from the base, they looked white and unfit as though seeing the light for the first time. They peered at me through specs balanced on their fat cheeks. Their padded parkas appeared too heavy for them. They were out of breath and reached for another fag with shaky hands. Is this the culture that these Eskimos are being educated for, I thought, and I knew which I considered superior.

It was trading day at the co-op so I bundled Rory into his carry-bag on my back and Rona's new friend, Kumie, told me where to go. She wore a duffel petticoat under her scarlet parka, completely lined with white fox fur and her kamiks were embroidered with a design of pink and blue plants. The co-op was solid with people. On the shelves were condensed milk and blue jeans. Above the clicking, short syllables of Eskimo, I heard the unmistakable soft accent of the West Highlands of home!

"Chust one moment," said the man in charge politely to his Eskimo clients and rose to shake my hand. "William McKenzie is my name." He had retained his old world social graces in spite of leaving Loch Carron as a young lad. I asked him why he had left his glen. "Because it had nothing for me but to be a ghillie to an English laird." He told me of the rainy day when he was fourteen that had brought about his decision to go. The Laird, a London stockbroker, was paying his annual visit to his land, and wanted a shoot, so William set off with him up the hill. They hadn't gone far when, "William!" roared the stock-broker, and threw the boy his overcoat to carry. Fifty feet higher up the heathered slope, "William!" he shouted again and threw off his tweed jacket. The sky cleared, "William!"— and the laird threw across his silver whisky flask, then eventually the telescope, which the boy had been longing to get his hands on all day. He immediately put down his heavy load and gazed through it, fascinated. The sun shone as he put all his attention into the instrument. He grew hotter and dozier. He slid down behind a boulder. He went to sleep! Meanwhile, the big-game hunter strode ten miles ahead over the hill, never looking back. At last he saw a stag. But suddenly, he found he had no ghillie, no gun—and worst of all no flask! William woke up to a tirade. "William! you Scottish peasant, you — — —." The following day he noticed an advertisement in the *Inverness Courier* for a "gentleman adventurer" with the Hudson Bay Company, and he sailed for Canada in a few weeks.

I asked William's advice about a pair of kamiks for Sandra, as we wanted her to feel at home among the locals, and he showed me how to spot a good skin. William could identify the source of the pelts by fingering the skins. A woman came up and handed me just the size of boot I wanted. The design was of vertical pieces of skin, minutely stitched together. This was the male design; women were supposed to wear boots with horizontal lines, but our feet were of masculine size compared to the little females of the North. "Don't buy from her," said William. "Those boots will stink in a few days. That woman doesn't bother to chew all the fat out of the skin before sewing it together. Here is a pair from Grise Fjord. The design of the duffel inners is purer there—not too influenced by Catholic missionaries, who encouraged daisies and pretty Indian signs and symbols, quite out of character to the matter-of-fact Eskimo."

An Eskimo boy came up to us with a model of an igloo made of ceiling tiles, probably, I realised, swiped from the base. A new culture after all! I lifted the lid. Three minute figures were inside, one mending a harpoon, one handling a baby and one scraping a skin. Owing money to the Government co-op, the boy wanted to trade his work of art for some food.

"I'll take it, Deuteronomy," said William, "but you must bring in three seal carcases if you still want a tin of Nescafé and three of powdered milk, plus those tins of chopped ham and all that bubble chewing-gum."

William stuck a label for thirty dollars on the model and placed it on the shelf. An American from the base would buy it at that exorbitant cost without question. Who was diddling who I was not quite sure.

The hunting around Resolute was not good. "Why do they

live here then?" I asked William. He explained that the village
was artificial and had been founded only in the 1940s by the
Government. Two other settlements had been uprooted and
their inhabitants dumped down here, some official having the
vision of the Eskimos manning the weather stations and making
the met. observations. This had never come about: the
Eskimos were now hooked to the co-op and it was too late to
replace them in their own territory.

The anthropologist Guppy's words came into my mind.
He was speaking of the Wai Wai Indians of Guyana, but he
could have been referring to Resolute. "Integration means the
destruction of one culture by another, and the turning of one
tribe into serfs for the dominant one."

And now there was oil. Instead of an asset to the impover-
ished Eskimos, would it be the cause of their final destruction?
The important oil strike by British Petroleum at Prudhoe Bay,
northern Alaska, had sparked off a multi-million-pound oil
rush to Canada's arctic islands. The target area is the hundred
thousand square miles of the Sverdrup basin, and geophysicists
are ninety-nine per cent certain that billions of tons of oil lie
under the thousands of feet of permafrost on several islands of
the group, and under the thick ice of the polar shelf. Pan
Arctic, the big Canadian Government-subsidised group of
companies, had started operations on Melville Island. Among
others in the dash to make a strike were Gulf Oil of France,
Sun Oil, Global Marine, Mobil and Imperial of America. They
all seemed to agree that the oil field could well extend to a
larger area than that in the Middle East. Experiments had
been carried out both with rigs which stand on the sea bed and
those which will sit on top of the ice. In the case of the latter,
ice-freezing chemicals and machinery would keep the ice at a
uniform thickness all the year round. Plans were being made to
ship out the oil in giant tankers with reinforced bows which
would bulldoze their way through the ice of the North-West
Passage, using the same route as Franklin and his companions
had searched for so long ago. Other bright ideas included pulling the oil in giant bladders behind submarines, or even a
pipeline on the sea bed. It all seemed impossible as I looked out
of the window to the desolate scene outside.

There was a general move, in the crowd at the co-op, towards the door. Dumpy mothers in red anoraks were hurrying through the grey light, in their soft kamiks, up the steep slope towards a spanking new shed-like building on the official "road" along from the flag beside the school. I followed, slithering in my clumsy boots on the glass-like surface. How did they keep their feet? Inside the shed, Eskimos were stacked neatly against the walls, silently watching, the children subdued. This was, to use Canadian Government language, the "Nursing Station". Doling out anti-T.B. pills was a tall hygienic young man. "My name is Ingo. I come from East Germany. I trained in Liverpool," he stated, offering no explanation. He spoke impeccable, text-book English. I watched fascinated, as he went down the line opening mouths, tapping teeth, and peering into eyes. His patients offered no resistance, mutely and limply bending to his authority. A pong from the sealskin kamiks wafted through the thickening air, so the nurse reached for his aerosol.

"I invite you to use my facilities," said Ingo, gesturing over his shoulder. "The Government fills my water tank." I edged past the crowd and looked into an inner room. A bath, and a lavatory seat below which protruded the frill of a green plastic bag. It was all spanking clean, but I wondered how Ingo came to terms with the plastic bag!

The twilight had slipped into dark as I left the Nursing Station and gingerly picked a foothold in the slope above our house. "Watch, Mum," yelled a voice as a figure shot towards me at breakneck speed. It was followed by another, faster, and another and another. School over, the village children were tobogganing on one curved runner nailed to a cross piece, one foot and both hands extended, as in a ballet poise.

"Pictures tonight, can we go, can we go?" chanted Robin, Bruce and Rona as we all pushed into the warmth of the hut. "You'll say it's too late," said the children, "but nobody goes to bed here except us."

"All right, but I'll come too," I replied.

The most substantial building in the village was a large garage which held the Government's Bombardier.

At 9 p.m. I joined the trail of villagers heading in its

direction. The temperature was minus 30 degrees. The Eskimo women ambled along, gossiping, as they only do in Glasgow on a rare balmy summery day. Inside the bare barn-like garage some of us sat on benches carried over from the school, the rest on the floor. Pudluk bustled about with an air of knowing what he was doing. He was official projectionist. Sudlavenik, as village elder, was involved too. After half an hour, between them, they eventually managed to coincide picture and screen. Sound and picture were more difficult to control and as an hour had gone by, the audience decided, good naturedly, to put up with the cowboys' voices drifting some way behind their galloping horses as they charged across the screen and off on to the wall behind. The woman beside me chewed. Then I realised that all the women were making use of the time, gazing intently at falling indians while they prepared sealskin for sewing. Pudluk could not work the projector with one hand, so every time he wanted another cigarette the film ground to a halt while he lit up. Nobody minded the interruptions. We had five films altogether, all American, all of which were equally crude. For a European the entertainment value was nil. The Eskimos in the village had all come, but how much of the message was getting through? Surely some little Canadian clerk could have selected a programme more worthy of the audience to send on a plane all the way up to Resolute. Perhaps Canadian officials have been brain-drained themselves by their U.S. neighbours to enjoy this type of drivel.

Bruce's eighth birthday fell the following day. "I'll bring a cake up to the school," I said, quashing his idea of a conventional party in our little Eskimo hut. It was T.B. pill time as Sandra and I entered the school bearing a rather queer cake and a billy-can of violet jelly. We kicked off our boots beside the pile at the door. The round-faced children were queuing up, waiting to receive their prophylactic. A birthday is unimportant to the Eskimo. Babies are swopped, girl for boy, or handed on as a regular occurrence and no one knows today's date, let alone that of the child's birth. Noah's mother was an old crinkly woman—of thirty or so. She had a baby last week—a girl—so had handed it round to another family who only had three boys. She herself had adopted someone else's baby boy in exchange.

The schoolteacher spoke no Eskimo. Excited by the sight of the cake, one child expressed himself in his own language. He was firmly slapped. The older children's class were "doing" English. A poem of a boy fishing in a stream with a willowy rod on a summery afternoon was chalked on the board, and the Eskimo kids intoned the garbled words. Had the teacher forgotten that this was not suburban Montreal? Eskimos lucky enough to be born in Greenland are taught in the local language and school books are illustrated and printed with their environment in mind. A Danish teacher has to attend a course in Eskimo culture and tradition, and signs on for three years. He goes to Greenland because he is genuinely interested in the way of life. The contrast with what is offered the North American Eskimos was pathetic. Meanwhile, I noticed Bruce, with a dead-pan face, corrupting the English lesson by teaching the boys a rude version of "Happy Birthday to You".

Rona's class was in the next room. Big Kumie of about fifteen sat on one side and a round little child on the other. They were learning the alphabet, complicated by the fact that missionaries had introduced symbols for sounds as in the Red Indian language. Kumie had to unlearn writing her name with two of these and substitute five letters. Cake and jelly were gobbled up all round.

That night I took up Ingo's offer of a bath. It was marvellous to leave our scruffy little hut and enter the spotlessly clean "Nursing Station" and strip off my nine layers of clothes in the warmth. My body looked strange, leggy and white. I had not seen it for five weeks. The water ran with gurglings and hissings. I sank in delightedly. I balanced Ingo's brand-new copy of *The Trial of Stephen Ward* on my knee. It was marvellous. I lay there for an hour. Reluctantly, I pulled the plug. A thick black rime was exposed as the water ran out. As I opened cupboards searching for Vim I became aware of a heavy waft of stink. I looked into the passage. Grey water was lapping along in a little wave. I paddled into the main room. The basin was overflowing with grey water, a thick scum on the surface. The smell was appalling. I rushed back to the bathroom, inches deep in water oozing out of cupboards and bubbling out from under the lino on the floor. My pile of clothes was floating! So was

Ingo's new book. Naked, I opened the main door and started to bale the flood into the perishing cold night. Overcome with guilt I could think of nothing else to do. I worked frantically and overcame the water, but was left with the smell and the dirt. Appalled, I surveyed the damage. It took me three hours to clean it up.

"Oh," said Ingo, when I summoned up courage to confess. "You should always drain the cesspit before you commence your ablutions."

Our hut was now littered with little piles of food that Hugh insisted he was "organising". In spite of weight, we could not skimp on our rations. Food was of supreme importance; starvation is well known by arctic expeditions. At the end of the American Greely's expedition to Ellesmere Island in the 1880s, six out of twenty-five people remained alive; the rest had died of hunger. The survivors had lived off seaweed and minute shrimps. There would not even be that to help us to keep alive. Scott's party's loss of strength, and vulnerability to cold, was caused by inadequacies in their food. A great deal of scientific work has been put into diet in the intervening years and more concentrated foodstuffs developed. Hugh had spent three years in the Antarctic questioning how men react to their diet, what gave them energy, what helped to keep out the cold. The rations we were taking on our journey were based on his experience. Such knowledge is important for undeveloped nations, since protein is expensive and, in the interests of economy, one wants to give each person just sufficient protein for health. Does a hard working coolie require more calories but the same amount of protein as his wife? Our journey to the Pole was an ideal way to test protein requirements in hard working conditions, and we undertook a research project under the auspices of the International Biological Programme. Our rations were all packed on a one-day one-man basis and each of us were to list anything uneaten after each meal. The rations were divided into twelve days on one diet of high protein and twelve days on low protein—the calorie intake remaining constant. All the time our urine volume was to be logged and a few cubic centimetres stored in test tubes and brought home so that later, at Glasgow University, it could be analysed for nitrogen content.

Protein contains nitrogen and in this way, by knowing the intake and output, a balanced survey could be carried out to find out if we were deteriorating—that is, losing more nitrogen than we were gaining. The protein in our food was in the form of dehydrated meat. The rest of our rations consisted of oats, biscuits, a great deal of butter, powdered milk, dried soup and very little else. No luxuries. Food would be a fuel, nothing more. One man's rations for a day weighed $2\frac{1}{2}$ pounds. The full weight of food in the sledge was 440 pounds.

We tucked into a supper of seal stew. Black, strong and delicious: heaps of thick gravy and big chunks of meat. I had bought it from William at the store, as a final gesture to civilisation.

CHAPTER THREE

WE WERE ALL busy writing, huddled round the stove, on the evening of February 21st, when the message came. "Be ready for take-off 6 a.m." Speechless, I sat for a second, then went through to our room, sank on to the bed, buried my head in my hands and cried. Robin, Bruce and Rona lay in a heap in sleeping bags, like a litter of piglets, fast asleep. Rory was face down in his cardboard box cot—relaxed as only sleeping babies can be, tiny hands outstretched. I could not bear the thought of leaving them. The last thing I wanted to do was to go to the North Pole. Why had I said that I did? Why were we doing it the hard way, without planes to back us up? Years of planning had sped past—reading and writing about the North Pole—and, with a sickening jolt, I realised that time had run out and now only the journey itself lay before us.

The feverish activity of Hugh and Roger broke through my tears. It was 10 p.m.—only eight hours to go. Food and equipment still had to be packed. We were taking so very little with us that each item was of supreme importance. Nothing could be forgotten. Sandra and I relooked at the billy-cans, Primus stove and checked the matches. At 5 a.m. I realised that I would have to call it a day and get dressed. I fetched my bag stuffed with clothes and emptied it on the floor. I took off all I had on—there was no time left for even one quick last wash. We had given endless thought to the question of keeping warm when it is 60 degrees below and yet we must be able to move easily in lightweight clothes. First, I pulled on pure wool long-johns and vest, then an extremely light cashmere jersey, knitted for us in South Harris. Then my Hellyhensens—a Norwegian suit of nylon fur woven on cotton, the fur inside. Another light wool sweater on top, the idea being that a layer of warm air would be trapped between it and the nylon fur. Next came a thin but windproof anorak with a closely fitting hood. In the front we had made a "muff" which we thought would be useful to prevent binos and cameras from freezing up. The top layer of the outer windproof anorak was made of material which was woven with cotton in one direction and nylon in the other, very strong and well tried on many a mountain top. I had sewn wolverine fur around the front of the hood which came out far in front of my face, thus adopting the Eskimo technique of trapping warm air which one would breathe, so warding off frost-bite from one's face. Our boots were Japanese, heavy, but made of insulated plastic material and guaranteed to keep us warm up to minus 80 degrees. They had been evolved for the Japanese Himalayan expedition and Roger had worn an identical pair on his dog sledge journey from Greenland to Ellesmere Island, with Peter Peary, when they had crossed Smith Sound in the early spring. Two layers of windproof trousers, Hellyhensen socks and gloves and a pair of long-cuffed leather gauntlets completed the job. I looked like a spaceman as I stood in front of the stove. I did not realise then that the next time I took these clothes off, I would be standing in exactly the same spot.

I tried not to hear the rumbling of the Bombardier. But I could not make time stand still. "Come on, come on," Hugh urged as I stood riveted to the floor. I would have to wake the children. I could not creep off and let them face the realisation in the morning that we had gone.

I went through to their rooms. I shook Robin. He looked at me and his face slowly crumpled as he saw me in all my clothes. "Mum, oh Mum," said Rona, clutching at my neck. Bruce just gazed at me with great tears silently pouring down his cheeks. I kissed Rory. He woke up and his fat little face broke into a great smile. This was the worst moment. I was cheating him. The others knew we were off.

I had to go. I fumbled out of the door into a biting wind and closed it firmly behind me. The cold was bitter and in the dark I could just make out Hugh and Roger loading our sledge on to the roof of the Bombardier. I tried not to look at the window of the hut until I was inside the cab. Three faces were pressed against it, noses squashed, crying with great sobs, tears freezing in blobs on the glass. But behind them I saw Sandra competently busy with breakfast, Rory on her hip wondering what all the fuss was about.

We roared off into the night. The driver, George Jost, a VIP at the Base, became confused among the huts, and mixed us up with the sleeping span of husky dogs. They unwound and stood up to shake out their fur, as if they were geese. I huddled back in my wadding of clothes and cut off mentally, so as not to think of my darling Rory and the rest. I allowed myself to cry silently until we reached the base. What seemed to me a minute plane was standing ready for us out on the runway, lit by one brilliant searchlight beam. It resembled a Woolworth's model made by Robin—badly stuck together at that. Friendly hands handed up our loads; we had far too much. Was this really going to fit on our one sledge? It practically filled the plane!

Ken, the Mountie, was coming for the ride. He stood beside the plane, looking as big and firm and strong as ever. The *Daily Telegraph* reporter, John Mossman, ambled into the light, looking as if he had a hangover, which he did. At vast expense, the *Telegraph* had also sent a top American photographer, Fred, to immortalise our departure. As we would be setting off in pitch darkness, we rather grudged him his fee. He looked highly organised, cameras stowed away in little boxes in each hand and neat bags slung round his neck. I knew his pockets would be full of "instant energy powders" and high calorie pills. Mix with water and hey presto, a three course meal!

A crate of Coca Cola and a box of Tom Collins were handed into the plane. "Going to stop at Eureka," explained Fred, who knew all that was going on. "A Joint Arctic Weather Station, or JAWS, for short."

Weldy Phipps' woolly dog bounded up, grabbing scarves and gloves in its slobbering jaws. It sunk its teeth into Hugh's left hand as he aimed it a clout. Heavens, I thought, the entire expedition, all £10,000 worth, is to be jeopardised by a stupid dog. Fred lined us up for a photo. "Back a bit," he directed me. A split instant before I obeyed, out of the corner of my eye, I caught sight of the propellers beginning to turn a few inches behind my head!

"Quick, quick, all aboard!" shouted fat stocky Weldy himself, as he jumped out of a truck, that had brought him from his caravan, and straight up into the cockpit, one foot only touching the ground.

I climbed up the ladder and we all sat down in a neat little row, Indian file. I felt frightened of the littleness of the plane. No going back now. The door was firmly shut. As if a car on a Sunday afternoon's jaunt, the plane started, nonchalantly ambled over the snow, speeded up and we were off. I was engulfed in that sinking feeling. It was as dark as pitch. Higher, there was a bit of light in the sky. It was dawn somewhere.

It was difficult to separate the dull white sea from the dull white land. It went on for ever. Fred delved in his pockets and produced a thermometer—minus 22 degrees! It was bitter cold in the plane. Ken saw to us all. He blocked up the ventilator gushing icy air down my neck; he handed along a plastic mug of hot coffee; he offered me a sardine sandwich. The plane droned on. Warmth came at last from the heater. Fred held out his thermometer again. Still minus 22 degrees. He looked perplexed. I asked John for some paper and wrote to my children. I had never meant to make them unhappy, but I had to attempt this journey. Could they understand?

"Interesting to know how far you make in a week," shouted Ken. "We have a map on the Arctic Circle Club wall."

"Very interesting," I said, not bothering to shout back.

It was vaguely light by eight. There were mountains below. Black rock and white snow. Slight tinges of blue. That was the only colour. No green, or pink or red. I hated the colourlessness of it all.

The plane droned on over the uninhabited islands. It crossed my mind that it was a relief there was so much space left in the world; five hours of it: unclimbed mountains and glaciers for my children to explore. I had always worried that there would be nothing left for them. I sat back in my seat and thought of all the troubles that now lay behind us.

Everything is against an expedition. Government departments consider one a nuisance and try to dissuade one as much as possible. An "explorer's licence" must be obtained to come North. It is difficult to procure and one of its provisos is an insistence on the use of a radio. We had carried no wireless on

any previous expedition. We had spent six months in Spitzbergen without one—had buried ourselves in South American
jungle with no contact with the outside world. We had travelled
right across Greenland without weighing ourselves down with
one. We much preferred to be free agents. Hugh, in fact, considered a radio actively dangerous. If one fails to come up on a
radio schedule the outside world expects one to be in dire distress
and precipitates a search and rescue operation when all one
really needs is to have a little time. No one made Nansen take a
radio, I thought. Nor did he have the political difficulties that
had faced us. The area that we wished to travel in is considered
of importance by the departments of Defence of both Canada
and the U.S.A., and it was difficult to get the idea across to
them that we were travellers and not spies.

There was a bright light in the sky—a silver crescent moon
hung in front of us with Venus close beside like a Christmas
decoration. "Ellesmere," Hugh shouted over his shoulder.
Below was a river of ice. It was Nansen Sound. I stared with
excitement. This was Sverdrup's country. He was Nansen's
companion across Greenland and had then skippered the *Fram*
when Nansen had taken it into the ice as a base for his attempt
on the Pole. Later Sverdrup returned to explore the creeks and
crannies and to map the coast of Ellesmere.

It had been Sverdrup's route that Roger had followed to this
coast, on his journey from Greenland with Wally Herbert.
Sverdrup had nursed the *Fram* up the sound between the east
coast of Ellesmere and Greenland, past Lifeboat Cove, where
the American steamer *Polaris* was stranded in a sinking condition on October 16th 1872, with fourteen men aboard. The
Polaris was with Hall's expedition, but the leader himself had
died suddenly of arsenic poisoning, while his party was wintering in "Thank God" harbour, which was as far north as any
ship had penetrated up the channel between North Ellesmere
and Greenland. On the day before she was stranded on the
homeward journey, the *Polaris* had dumped the rest of the party,
consisting of twelve men, two women and five children, on to
the ice, along with most of the provisions, clothing and boats;
the ship had suffered much from pressure, and was leaking

from every seam. While everyone was busy organising the Eskimo families, the ship's moorings gave, and she was carried away in a strong breeze. It was ten in the evening, dark, and nothing could be done by the horrified castaways to save the situation. For the entire winter they drifted about on their mobile icefloe, and only lived to tell the tale because an Eskimo, Hans Hendrik, was with them. Hans had his kayak, and harpooned seals to keep the whole party alive until April 30th, when they were picked up near Newfoundland. They had drifted from latitude 78°30′ to 53°30′! In the meantime, the fourteen men carried away in the *Polaris* wintered in Lifeboat Cove. They built two boats out of the woodwork of the vessel, and, once spring had come, set out in them for home! They rowed right along the coast of Greenland until, on June 23rd, they were picked up by an astonished whaler in Melville Bay.

Sverdrup himself wintered for his first year just south of Greely's fatal camp site, and called the sheltered little bay, "Fram's Haven". During the winter months, Sverdrup made up his mind to attempt to cross Ellesmere Land, as he called it, and reach the west coast. He set out on April 17th, with four men and five dog-teams, relying on living off the land *en route*. There were plenty of musk ox, although the dogs tended to chase just the ones that the explorers decided were too fierce to be hunted! Sverdrup found himself expending more energy defending his dogs than shooting food for himself! Sverdrup, like Nansen, enjoyed himself under any contingency, and once fell off the sledge from laughing too much, only just struggling to his feet in time to fling himself on to the next sledge as it flew past.

As Sverdrup approached the watershed of Ellesmere, he saw, far away on the horizon, a chain of Alpine like mountains, with sharp crags and snow-covered peaks. The way looked easy, but his party was suddenly brought to a halt by an impassable canyon, running due west. Eventually they found a way round, but could only make progress on foot, with no sledge. After a hard journey, they reached a mountain they called The Thumb, and were struggling round the lower shoulder when suddenly they found themselves on a sharp ledge, with sides falling perpendicularly into water. "Such a surprise was it, and so grand the panorama which opened out to view, that we burst out into a cheer," wrote Sverdrup in his account of the expedition. Right beneath them lay the fjord, broad and shining, without so much as a flake of snow on it, only crystal clear ice that looked like a huge fairy mirror. Opposite was a great chain of mountains, with snow-filled clefts and black abysses, jagged peaks and wild precipices.

These were the mountains on which we now looked down.

Black dots below came into focus and I realised we were losing height. Eureka! We landed into our own blizzard as Weldy put the propellers into reverse to bring us to a quick halt. We all clambered out and hastily entered a hut. Ten men lived here—all alone. Five American and five Canadian.

"Sure, we're still friendly," answered an elongated negro to my question. He was making bread, tossing a wodge of dough from one white palm to the other. There were a few pin-ups on the wall, not particularly lush, and a bowl of red plastic anemones. We drank coffee from a machine. Press the button and out popped a sterile cupful. I felt it was socially incumbent for me to take some clothes off to show the men that my shape was not entirely pillow. The men were all for us. I felt their warmth, and the contrast from Resolute. These hoped we would succeed. The boss, from the deep South, gave me a hat: khaki, with furry ear-flaps. "Wear it for us," he said.

"Sure," I answered. "Just what I needed."

Weldy had his ear to the Eureka radio. "Alert won't let me land with you aboard," he said, perplexed, to Hugh. "And I might need to, if we can't get in at Ward Hunt. The weather's brewing up. Not enough fuel to get back here." Alert is alleged to be another weather station down the coast of Ellesmere, facing Greenland; as the crow flies, it is only one hundred miles from Ward Hunt. We did know, however, that ninety-two American servicemen were stationed there and that it was very much involved with an atomic weapon and all that jazz.

"I wish you stupid Americans would stop playing at soldiers," I stormed at the Eureka radio man. He looked at me, slightly hurt, horn-rimmed specs trembling on his nose. I could not imagine him even fighting the Vietcong. What a contrast to the nineteenth-century expeditions, I thought. The Royal Navy had actually paid explorers, not frustrated them as the American services were doing to us now. Peary himself received a rear admiral's salary! The radio clicked into activity once more.

"Repeat: The Simpson party must not, on any account, put down at Alert."

I felt like the little girl uninvited to the party. Hugh did not argue. He doesn't usually. He saved his energy to persuade Weldy to gamble on landing at Ward Hunt, and we were off again in minutes. There was magnificent scenery below, of arched ridges of mountains, sweeps of glaciers. Looking out into that jumble of passes and peaks I realised that it was obviously easier to go on to the Pole than to try to come back! I looked at my watch. Only three-quarters of an hour left in the friendly, snug little plane. A mountain below now looked exactly like Mam Sodhail, north of Glen Affric. A lozenge-shaped lochan, practically encircled by a steep escarpment, nestled in its southern slopes. My mind on home, I wondered if we should have sent the children there. No, I reiterated to myself. It was a privilege for them to live with the Eskimos. There would be none left when they grew up.

"One last message?" said John Mossman hopefully, bending over my shoulder, notebook poised. I had no chance to reply. We were there.

CHAPTER FOUR

We were completely on our own. If we had forgotten anything it was just too bad. We would not let ourselves down, nor the *Daily Telegraph*. I was sure of that, but suppose any of our equipment failed? Having no chance of re-supply by air-drop, there was absolutely nothing we would be able to do about it. Peter Freuchen—an old Greenland hand—said that in the Arctic one's job is accomplished against a back-drop of continued struggle—continued struggle for existence. A great deal depends on the individual and his failure may be as fatal to his companions as to himself. No man should go to the Arctic before he is sure of himself.

There was no more time for moralising. Hugh and Roger were already struggling to push their arms through the harness straps, then hook themselves on to the karabiner at the end of the rope attached to the sledge.

"Which way's north?" I said as I followed suit. Hugh waved his arm in a vague direction away from Mount Walker.

"Well, there's the Plough," he said. The moon hung slightly to the right of the belt of seven stars. We set our faces towards it, bracing ourselves for the first steps of our 500-mile or so journey.

Friction we knew would be our greatest enemy. In spite of the polyethelene runners of our sledge, we expected to have much trouble in pulling it across the snow at the very low temperatures that we were going to meet. So, very gingerly, we all took the weight of the sledge and tried to edge it forward. To my great surprise, it actually moved! Across the lake, then down a little slope. Rocks showed through in one spot and I bent down and kicked three pebbles loose, which I stowed away in my pocket, thinking of the kids.

"The most northerly point of land in the Americas," I said, feeling the occasion was worthy of note.

There is a skirt of smooth shelf-ice attached to Ward Hunt Island and it was at the edge of this that we camped for that first night. On the move I had been quite warm but as soon as I unclipped my karabiner from my harness, I felt the cold moving in. My hands became clumsy as I held one end of the tent bag while Hugh yanked out the bundle of red material. Parts of my body I had not been aware of before began to hurt: my left cheek, where frost had joined it to the ice encasing the fur around my anorak hood, my finger-tips, my nose. I looked about us. Flat greyness. Nothing. Three of us and one tiny sledge looking microscopic in the vast surroundings.

When the tent was up, loneliness vanished. It gave the illusion that we now had somewhere to go. Roger fixed the guys to our ice axes while I kicked up loose snow to fill the billy-can. Hugh scrambled in through the sleeve entrance and began to assemble the Primus. In a few moments I could hear the most important sound of our limited world—the roar as the little stove sprung into life. I now handed Hugh the tent floor. Slabs of two-inch thick polystyrene, sandwiched in nylon material in case it crumbled with wear and tear.

"Minus 38," said Roger, holding his met. thermometer outstretched. I crouched down, and elbowed my way in beside Hugh and the welcome warmth. One candle lit the tent as I undid the first box of food. We opened the ration bags and extracted the cubes of dehydrated meat of matchbox size. I crumbled them into the billy-can of snow and stirred until the contents began to boil. We were warm and cosy and all seemed right with the world. Hugh crouched in one corner among his test tubes and box of medical research equipment. I sat cross-legged in the middle with the Primus, and Roger sat by the door. His longer legs curled round him in an untidy knot. We all focused our attention on the billy-can of stew. When ready, we slurped it up at high speed. Our one sleeping bag entirely covered the tent floor and seemed plenty big enough that night as Hugh and I slithered in from one end and Roger from the other. "Going to bed" meant taking off our boots. Roger's feet came up to my face, but I did not mind because his legs gave me added insulation from the outside. Once in the bag, Hugh turned the Primus off. The silence overwhelmed me. It seemed as if nothing else lived in the whole world; there was a total suspension of time and life. I snuggled down beside Hugh.

Actually I was supremely happy. There is something marvellous about travelling like nomads, everything that was needed for life on the sledge.

"Travelling is a fundamental instinct," said Hugh, his mind on the same plane. "Like hunting or sex, or competition and that is why I find my satisfaction in it difficult to explain."

I travelled for personal experience—a longing to be part of the scene and to prove my self-sufficiency. For this one has to be alone. I remembered what Nansen wrote on the first evening at sea in the *Fram* on his attempt to reach the Pole. "It was like balm to the soul after all the turmoil and friction with crowds of strangers." I felt exactly the same. It was great to be alone, but for a few highly selected companions.

It was pitch-dark in the tent now, no question of reading our one book—Dickens' *Martin Chuzzlewit*—or writing my notes. We had two "long-life" candles which must be reserved for cooking and for Hugh's research. I consoled myself by remembering that Churchill never kept a diary as he reckoned that one was always pessimistic in the evening and in the morning one must get on with living the next day. The tent floor was comfortable to lie on and I felt completely insulated from the ice below. If Hugh turned over in bed, I had to, too, and if Roger bent his knees, I became the shape of a Z-bend. But I soon sank into that marvellous sleep that goes with physical effort and a day's work well done.

I stirred to a scuffling noise but felt far too tired to do anything about it and slept again. A glimmer of light told us that it was morning. 4 a.m. Maximum daylight would be 11 a.m., local time, so we had to gear our routine to that. I lifted my head, then hastily hid it in the sleeping bag as an avalanche of hoar frost crystals showered down on my face.

Moving as little as possible Hugh stretched out an arm and lit the Primus. In a moment the hoar frost evaporated and we could sit up. "It's weight that's going to get us," said Hugh. "I have been thinking about it all night. We must cut down on weight."

"I am prepared to tear some pages out of my nautical almanac," Roger said generously, and immediately attacked it with his knife. Pages of advertisements for fast ship repairs in

Athens went first, then the tables for January. "Just smashing, throwing away days like this," he said and February went before I could stop him. "High water at Avonmouth, salvage stations in the Mediterranean. Interested?" asked Roger, his teeth glinting in the candle light. My contribution was my toothbrush and the cover of my notebook. Ruefully I looked at the photo of Rory that I had slipped between the pages, and added that too. Anything that did not contribute to forward progress must go. There was to be only one interest in our lives —to reach the Pole.

The weight on the sledge was 902 pounds; 440 pounds of this was food for sixty days—95 pounds of it was ten gallons of paraffin. Camping equipment accounted for 47 pounds, and the radio and generator 86 pounds. We each had a personal bag. Hugh's was empty, mine practically, whereas Roger's bulged. We queried this but he insisted that everything inside was essential either for his navigation or for mending the sledge. Scott reckoned that 180 pounds per man was a heavy load for a manhauling journey, that is 540 pounds for three. We were carrying 350 pounds more but we needed every ounce. Our temperatures would be lower than Scott's and we calculated that one gallon of paraffin would last only six days. Nansen reckoned on a gallon for thirty days, but he was made of tougher stuff than us. Both Scott and Nansen had a high ratio of edible weight to static—our balance was on the other side, owing to the radio, its generator and fuel. What could we do? Modern line of thought insisted that we take it, and the news-paper supporting us expected reports from the field.

Roger struggled to untie the tent door. It was a sheet of ice, our warm breath had frozen on it. He put his arm out to scoop snow into the billy-can and let in an icy blast of cold air. Breakfast was porridge, apple flakes, biscuits, butter and a glucose drink or tea. The cook provided hot water. I poured mine over the oats and apple flakes combined and added a huge dod of butter and my share of dry powdered milk. Lack of light made us slow. The polar historian, Hayes, said, "The Arctic winter is not the sledging season and its moonlight should be used with discretion." I knew what he meant as I fumbled in the tiny tent for my boots. They had acted as a pillow. Now they were frozen stiff and I held them one by one over the Primus to make them pliable enough to force my feet inside. Only one of us could stretch his legs at a time. Putting on one's boots had to be done in turns. Roger was out first, then Hugh. I ran my penknife along the side of the tent as I sat in my corner waiting for them to be ready. I chipped off half-inch thick wedges of ice which had formed a good two feet up the walls. I pulled my anorak hood well over my face before crawling into the gloom outside. A silent mistiness was hanging about as if waiting to envelop us if we made a mistake.

"There is no latitude for error," Nansen had said, "above 80° North."

Suddenly I noticed little fox footsteps. Their padded indentations encircled the tent. One food box was opened, the contents littered about. The fox had rifled through the lot but found nothing apparently good enough to eat. "Lucky we are not so fussy," I thought, as I packed the things back in the box.

Mount Walker loomed above us, just the shape of Edinburgh's Berwick Law. It rose from the centre of Ward Hunt Island and dominated the background. Slightly to the left were the magnificent mountains of North Ellesmere. In front of us there was just nothing but the smooth white of the shelf ice. I was warm in my Hellyhensens as we took down the little red tent, but I was conscious of the minus 45 degrees Fahrenheit as we fumbled with the rope to lash up the sledge. We reluctantly decided that we would now have to relay so we left half of our load alone on the snow and set off. Even so, we could only just move. We heaved and hauled on the harness and in a slow, slow shuffle, inched our way forward. At this temperature the sledge would not glide over the surface because of friction, caused by the fact that snow falls in small granules rather than flakes. The coefficient of friction apparently increases at low temperatures. Nobody seems to know quite why. With head down, my view was of yellow toe caps, an arc of snow and the tips of the wolverine fur which edged my hood as I struggled to put one foot in front of the other. I agreed with Nansen that "a world without sun is like a life without love". That is, pretty bleak. There was a silvery, hard light and here and there dark cold shadows projecting from a hummock of ice, the sides of which faintly reflected the twilight. It seemed as if we were walking in infinite space. I looked up for the first time. The north star was directly overhead.

We seemed to have been going for hours. I wondered how many. I felt all my energy had been drained from me. We seemed no nearer the pressure ridge that cut right across our horizon. I had to give up. What had kept other parties going? I remembered Scott's Captain Oates. The little party had passed the South Pole, but now big strong Seaman Evans was dead. The other four struggled on, but Oates was at the end of his tether. He had raw frost-bitten sores on his hands and feet. He was hungry and terribly tired. The food depots were sixty-five miles apart, with only a week's food in each. They would have to average nine miles a day if they were ever to get off the ice. Short of a man, it was beginning to dawn on their party that this was impossible. They were doomed. Oates was in despair. He turned to Dr Wilson, and said, "What shall I do? What shall I do?" Wilson, knowing the situation better than anyone, assessing it in his cool clear mind, answered Oates, "Slog on. Just slog on." Oates whipped his mind into control once more, and slogged on for another thirty days.

I knew that mental strength is far more vital than physical, but I was learning the lesson again. It does not matter how much muscle one has if there is no will-power to put it into effect.

As our sledge became lighter, when we ate into our food, it accumulated weight nearly as fast, from the sleeping bag which sopped up more water every night and turned to ice immediately it was taken out of the tent. The heat of the Primus never dried this moisture. It was becoming more and more of an effort to drag the bag through the tent door. The tent too became caked in ice, both walls. The ridge felt like a fat metal bar, inches in diameter. It took longer every day to force it into a shape manageable enough to lie on the sledge.

The only thing to do, as we slogged on, was to force one's mind thousands of miles away. I redecorated our house, planned alterations, and recited poems again and again. Oates used to provision his little yacht, calculating how much pickled herring he would need for various destinations. Cherry-Garrard invented a compact revolving bookcase to hold, not books, but pemmican, chocolate, biscuits, cocoa and sugar, that held a cooker on the top. It was always to stand at the ready to quench his hunger when he returned home. Garrard's party thought of restaurants, theatres, grouse moors and pretty girls.

We continued until 2 p.m. "I'm damered," said Roger, using his version of the Eskimo word for "that's enough". Immediately we loosened the lashings of the sledge and pulled out the yellow bag which contained the tent. The nylon crinkled in my fingers, hard and brittle in the minus temperatures. Each of us held one bamboo leg and set the tent on a hard patch of snow. Hugh slithered in to adjust the floor. Using the polystyrene was one of his more successful ideas. Its coefficient of thermal conductivity is only ·24 while that of granite for instance, is about 3. Roger and I set the 33-pound food boxes on the valance of flap around the tent, in case a wind should rise. Then, one slow look round for bears, and we turned back along our tracks for the other load.

The moon and Venus had now taken over the sky. It seemed vast and far more significant than normal. In three-quarters of an hour we reached our depot as opposed to three and a half hours on the outward trip. "Oh, how can we ever make 476 miles?" I thought, overwhelmed with despair. Plaisted, the mid-western American who had driven his snowmobile to the Pole the previous year, had 800 miles up on his mileometer on reaching his destination. Weldy's plane had refuelled and resupplied his party every few days, so they travelled very light and were able to detour round the difficulties.

I could not walk 800 miles, I thought, panic mounting in my throat. I heaved on my harness with the new load on the sledge, then one foot crunched through the breakable crust. I sank in halfway up to the knee. The sledge rode on top for a yard or two, then the runners broke through and all our heaving was to no avail. Roger untied and thrust on the back of the sledge and we moved again. No bears were in sight, nothing. The silent mountains were just visible behind; absolutely nothing in front but a barely discernible etched line separating sky and snow.

The tent at last; what a relief—like getting home. I was soon inside. Hugh lit the Primus in order to melt a billy-can of snow to fill the hot water bottle. This was to be our method of heating up the generator in order to run the radio. We thought it high time that we sent out a message to our newspaper that we were still alive. The *Telegraph's* final cable to us had read, not a wish of good luck, but "Do not give up before March 7th" which was the date they planned to print an article in their colour magazine!

The Primus suddenly failed. Surely it hadn't let us down already? We had plenty of spares luckily, but under usual camping conditions, a Primus runs for ever. Roger got out the plastic bag with bits and pieces inside. "I bought these spares in Dumfries," he said indignantly, as he began to wrestle with the nipple remover.

"These aren't Primus spares," I said, fingering the tools. "They are far too big."

We caught each other's eye, suddenly horrified. Our Primus was our source of life. Without heat we would very soon freeze in this environment. Roger worked away, and in a few minutes managed to fiddle in a new nipple and the Primus was soon going again. But I foresaw difficulties ahead. The hot water bottle system heated the generator beautifully and it started the first time Hugh pulled on its string. We could not bring the radio into the tent because of condensation, so Hugh crouched beside it outside and fiddled with the knobs while I held a match and read out the instructions for tuning to the appropriate frequency. At last we were ready. "Simpson mobile, Simpson mobile, Simpson mobile. Simpson mobile calling joint arctic weather stations, Simpson mobile calling JAWS. Can you hear us?" There was a second or two of silence. I could not imagine that anybody could possibly answer . . . crackle, crackle, crackle, crackle. "Eureka . . . crackle, crackle, spark, Eureka." It seemed like magic. My throat tightened and I began to cry. "A message from Sandra," suddenly the voice said, crystal clear, then it faded. Heavens, I thought, what has happened? A message from Sandra. Was Rory ill? Had Robin fallen off the roof? Was Rona pining for me? Had Bruce caught tuberculosis from his new friends? Hugh had his ear glued to the set. I shook him.

"For heaven's sake. What is it?"

He turned round: "Roger's new climbing boots have arrived. That's all."

I read our report into the wireless. "Message for *Telegraph*, London. February 22nd. All fine here: camped on most northerly tip of the Americas. Temperature minus 47, but snug in tent." By the time I had repeated each word three or four times I was so bored, as well as cold, that I eliminated the rest of our message. The radio man who received it at the other end seemed very matter of fact. I felt like shouting at him, "Do you realise that we are standing out here in a temperature of minus 47, 400 miles from you?"

"Okey, dokey," he said. "Over and out." And once more we were alone. I forced myself to move back into the tent. We were all hungry. As I bent over the Primus to prepare the meat-bar stew, a headache began to bore into my forehead. Roger was soon complaining too. Was it monoxide poisoning? I suddenly thought. Plenty of fresh air was entering the tent by Hugh's patent perforations between the ground sheet and the wall— his idea for combating just this contingency. But the yellow flame licked round the billy-can—a sure sign that the Primus was giving off Co and not Co_2. Hastily I turned it out.

Polar travellers are well aware of the dangers of carbon monoxide poisoning after the experience of André, the Swedish physicist, who planned to balloon to the North Pole. In 1899, he left Spitzbergen and was never heard of again. His party's bodies were discovered by a sealing vessel. They were in a tent and their diaries and photographs were recovered. The balloon had lost gas and come down north of Spitzbergen. They had a sledge but decided the Pole was impossible. So they set out to manhaul back home. The party was found with food and fuel on Kvitoya, an island to the east of Spitzbergen. There was no evidence of starvation and it was thought they died of carbon monoxide poisoning by leaving the Primus burning while they slept. Mawson, who led the Australian Antarctic expedition to Adelie Land in 1911, had the same experience. They had very high winds—the average speed for one month was forty knots —and found it difficult to pitch tents. A large depot was established a day's march from their base and it became their

Myrtle and Hugh Simpson pitching camp about 390 miles from the North Pole. Note polystyrene boxes and tiny mountain tent—their only one. Pressure ridge in background.

Myrtle Simpson and Roger Tufft manhauling northwards in chaotic pack-ice on the Arctic Ocean. March, 1969.

Myrtle Simpson and Roger Tufft manhauling in low drift over the polar pack. March, 1969.

habit to camp in a snow drift near the depot. The snow became iced over due to heating by a Primus and at least two of Mawson's sledging party suffered extreme carbon monoxide poisoning and were only just saved from death, their health being affected for the rest of their lives. I had had monoxide poisoning myself when camping at 20,000 feet in the Andes of Peru, in a snow-covered tent under cold conditions, when we had carefully closed up any source of ventilation. I remembered feeling ghastly, huddling into my sleeping bag, thinking I had soroche or altitude sickness. I struggled out of the tent to be sick, and my knees had given, and I had crumpled into the snow. It was only when my three companions joined me on the ground that we appreciated that the Primus was the cause of the trouble and not the height! Carbon monoxide combines with haemoglobin—the red material in the blood which carries oxygen. It does this two hundred times more easily than oxygen itself. This means that the blood is blocked from carrying the vital oxygen and death is rapid. The same situation holds when a potential suicide puts his head in the gas oven or a car is started in a garage. The victim dies a bright, healthy pink. I noticed our candle was tending to go out. Hastily I blew it out and we gobbled our stew in the dark. It was uncooked and cold.

Where would we be tomorrow, I thought, as we took our boots off for bed. Surely we would have reached the sea?

We met two hours of easy going the following day. The shelf ice tilted downhill towards a hard line across our path. As we drew near, I realised that it was a wall. Great slabs and chunks of ice were balanced on each other like a giant child's toy bricks. Incredible shapes were precariously perched on blocks. Henry Moore sculptures, as large as bungalows, were poised at prodigious angles. We halted under the ridge of ice and scrambled gingerly to the top. In front of us was the most fantastic view in the world. The polar pack. Away into the distance were blocks of ice tumbled and jumbled together in confusion—thin ribbons of leads, or separations, ran between the piled up ice. It looked like a city after an earthquake. I was mad with excitement for a minute or two before I appreciated exactly what lay before us. We had to find a way through that chaos; it looked impossible.

"Hurry up," yelled Hugh, completely unperturbed by what he had seen. He and Roger were setting back for the next load. The land had fallen away from us to right and left, with Mount Walker still close and dominating the scene. I wished I'd taken time to climb it when we were left by Weldy's plane. The land looked petrified, cold and dead, held in time, waiting for the kiss of the sun. The loneliness of northern Canada struck me. No happy Eskimo now lived along that coast. The last explorer who knew it well was Peary who travelled along the shelf ice in 1906 and 1909 in his attempts on the Pole.

"Let's stop for a brew," said Hugh, as we thankfully drew up outside the tent. I crawled in to light the Primus while the men loaded up the sledge. I took off my gloves and put my hand out for the stove. A searing pain shot up my arm like an electric shock. I had touched the metal and my fingers had stuck. I hastily pushed my hands back into the gloves. Cold had taken over now and I began to shake. All I had to do was to light one match in order to turn this refrigerator into a place of warm bliss but I just could not pluck up the courage to remove my glove and open the box. "I can't light the Primus," I shouted feebly to Hugh. "Why not?" His matter of fact voice spurred me on and in an instant I had the alcohol flaring into life. This warmed the paraffin in the stove and a glow spread over my face. The hoar frost melted off the fur around my hood and dripped into the flame which reacted with a yellow spurt. I pumped vigorously and the Primus roared out heat. Hot choco-late warmed the cockles of my heart. Hugh's and Roger's faces glowed in the flame. Already Roger looked like a pirate in a theatrical cast. Real ones could never look as scruffy as that. The stubble on his face, woollen hat to his eyes and toothy grin made him look wicked and ready for some rum. Hugh always looks right in his environment, learned among his professional colleagues, smart in his city suit, ready for a fling in his kilt, but now the true explorer looking for the Pole. An old English motto came to my mind: "He is happy whose circumstances suit his temper. But he is more excellent who can suit his temper to any circumstances."

It was inky dark when we set off again. I could only just make out our tracks if I peered at my feet. God, it won't move, I thought, putting all my strength on the haul. The temperature had dropped to minus 54. Hugh thrust at the back as Roger and I slithered one foot forward, then shuffled the other foot up. We moved in inches. Time rushed past as we crept on. Then suddenly I wondered if the load had fallen off. The sledge was following easily on behind.

"It's a bear pushing from the back," said Roger, and I looked round. We were going downhill! Venus was now supreme, hanging in the sky, her light gathering in intensity. On and on we went, showing a turn of speed at last. Our tracks mesmerised me, I felt as if in a dream. I actually fell over the depot before I realised that we had arrived.

"I so tired I need clock click," was what Rona used to say when taken hill walking. Now I felt the same. Hugh and Roger busily erected the tent while I stood gazing round about at the ghostly scene. It seemed warmer here under the sheltering arm of the wall of ice. At last we were on the brink of the pack and our journey had really begun. How did the ice become piled up like that? I wondered; when did it move? Where was the force that tossed hundred-ton blocks about as if confetti? I just did not know. Years of mountaineering and cross-country ski-ing had prepared me for the distance and the cold. But to walk over this frozen, moving sea was quite outside my experience. Or any other woman's for that matter. Peary took Eskimo women along on his journeys up the coast. He said "the presence of women is absolutely necessary to render the men contented." They were also supposed to mend the furs. But there have never been any women who have actually travelled on the polar pack. What a privilege, I thought. It does not matter if we do not reach the Pole, just to have this experience is enough.

It was snug in the tent and enthusiasm bubbled from us all with the prospect before us. The dehydrated meat was labelled "steak and kidney" and I pepped it up with oxtail soup. My mouth watered as I slurped it into the three bowls. "Lush," said Roger as he ladled it in. The sleeping bag was stiff with frozen condensation but once inside I was warm. I snuggled down into its double layer between the already snoring men.

CHAPTER FIVE

I stood at the top of a thirty-foot wall and slowly let out the rope that ran over my shoulder until Roger could reach the load attached to it. He perched in a foothold which he had chopped half way down the cliff. He looked like a smuggler as he reached up for the box, hoar frost all over his moustache and chin. He, in turn, handed the boxes to Hugh who shouldered them carefully, balanced on a knife-edge pile of ice blocks, and carried all that we owned in this icy world across to the only flat surface for miles around. I felt in an utterly new environment and a complete intruder as I scrambled down myself after one last look back over the smooth shelf-ice towards the land. Sledging was now impossible. Hugh carefully tied the radio on to his aluminium pack frame. Roger carried his precious box of navigation equipment and I loaded my own frame with two boxes of food. Carrying an ice axe to chop a route, Hugh set off first, hacking a way between the tottering piles of ice. The scenery was magnificent. Ice-caves and grottos, towering up-ended blocks and pillars made of little boulders of ice support-ing an immense chunk of floe on top, some thirty or forty feet high. Every chink between each piece of ice was filled with soft, dry snow, so to walk on the ice was imperative. I fell behind the others, enjoying the solitude, then suddenly remembered that we would not be alone in the polar pack. There were bears around.

The polar bear can run over the ice faster than man, as Nansen found out. He can climb rocks, icy ridges and also swim with great agility. His fur camouflages him perfectly and he stalks his prey in complete silence. He weighs at least 1,000 pounds and is afraid of nothing. He lives off seal, killing them with one downward swipe of his paw. I wasted time sweeping the horizon for a sight of one of these kings of the north. Each time I looked back over my shoulder, I lost my footing, and fell into a hole of soft snow. Nelson had been attacked by a bear, when a midshipman, off the coast of Spitzbergen and he had escaped by jamming his gun between its jaws. A Canadian scientist was recently dragged away in his sleeping bag by one on Melville Island, his horrified friend looking on, not daring to shoot; but I saw no movement or sign of life and began to be blasé about bears.

Hugh and Roger had found a flat pan just large enough for a tent. It had a soft covering of smooth snow. At one end chunks of ice rose up into fantastic shapes and forms. From the top I saw a redness in the sky over Mount Walker, now due south. To the north the Arctic Ocean appeared to be one mile above us, suspended on top of the horizon. This optical illusion is quite common in the north, like the mirage of an oasis in the desert. To and fro we went, back-packing the load to the floe. There was no rhyme or reason to this chaos of ice, just a higgledy piggledy tossing, as if due to a little child with a box of toys. I discovered a meandering path round one area of ice and felt like Alice in Wonderland as I strolled along. The scene was white and blue. By 3.30 p.m. everything was together and we decided to call it a day. I pottered about outside waiting until Hugh had the Primus roaring in the tent but I soon gave in and burrowed through the opening like a rabbit, leaving Roger to coil the sledge ropes and weight down the tent in case a wind sprang up during the night.

My tea tasted brackish that night, a sure sign we were camping on the sea. I dug in my personal bag for a tube of cream for my chapped face. It was frozen solid so I held it over the Primus to thaw. The plastic shell melted and ran into the palm of my hand, leaving the cream like a metal rod. Difficulties of life in the minus 40s and 50s were becoming apparent. Leaning back against the wall of the tent, I now found that I had frozen to the fabric and I had actually to pull myself away, leaving some strands of thread on the tent. The hoar frost was up to shoulder level now and the heat of the Primus would only lower it temporarily. During the day moisture formed on our clothes and condensed on our outer garments which were also now a mass of ice. They were so hard and stiff they would stand up by themselves and crackled and creaked when we moved. One cuff was so rough that it actually rubbed a sore on my wrist. Sitting in the tent, our windproofs slowly thawed out, but never dried, and froze again once the Primus was out. Each morning they were as suits of armour, and if taken off one needed help to prise one's way back in.

The next day we loaded our sledge with one-third loads and manhandled it through the pack. "This is the worst sledging in the world," said Roger, who had spent three years of sledging on the Antarctic ice in addition to his experience in the north.

I remembered the scorn that a Canadian Government official, Hattersley Smith, had thrown on our plans. Speaking for the Canadian Defence and Research Board in Ottawa, he had said that "the Simpson party will never do the first fifty miles to the Pole, due to excessive icing, pressure ridges, separation of party by moving ice, lack of paraffin and lack of experience of the polar pack." How awful if Hattersley Smith was right!

I was too busy to think of bears or Hattersley Smith for long, as we chipped at ice walls with our axes, clambered up ice blocks or balanced on boulder fields surrounded by deep soft snow. The spaces between the blocks were covered with thin deceptive layers of snow which gave under one's weight and sent one crashing through up to the waist. The sledge rallied behind us, twisting and bending like a snake. Relay of loads meant retracing steps again and again and I began to despair.

"Hey," shouted Hugh, who had scrambled to the top of yet another pile of ice. "Lead to the left."

We changed direction and thrust our way through an indescribable confusion of ice. Suddenly we came to the edge of what seemed to me to be a motorway cutting through a ruined town. I thought of Glasgow's devastated Charing Cross. The clearway stretched away to the north as far as I could see, absolutely straight and completely free of rubble. For the first time we unlashed our skis and pushed our feet into the loose bindings. The skis had been specially made for our journey by the same Norwegian firm that had supplied Nansen in 1888. He was the first to use skis on an expedition. Ours were of hickory and weighed only five pounds in spite of a hard wood edge. True cross-country skis would not have stood up to the distances

and surfaces that we expected to cover. Ours were both thicker
and wider in order to accommodate our broad boots.

Life was worth living after all. Our skis slid over the surface,
the sledge obediently trundled behind. The experience was
quite new to me and I felt like Moses leading the children of
Israel, crossing the Red Sea. High walls on each side cut off our
vision but I only wanted to see north so I did not mind. On we
went at high speed. Late in the evening we found a little camping site nestling under a pressure ridge at the end of our lead. I
took off my skis. Heavens, water was collecting in my footsteps.
I had not appreciated how thin a skin separated us from the
ocean's depth.

It was now the 27th. We had agreed to come up on our radio
once a week. Hugh tuned in while I wrote a message by candle-
light. The flame flared for a moment, flickered, then faded
with a hiss. I asked Roger to light me another but then realised
that this was our last! Hugh thrust the microphone at that
moment into my hand. "There's radio Isachsen," he said,
delighted to have made contact across the empty waste. "Quick,
they are waiting."

"I can't read my message," I yelled at him. "For goodness
sake make some light."

Hugh has a habit of doing a job thoroughly. I glanced over
my shoulder to see raging flames. "All well here," I read coolly
into the microphone, while I beat at the flames with one hand,
watching Hugh and Roger frantically trying to smother them
with hats and gloves. Without a tent in these latitudes, we
would die. We just had to put out the fire. The boys were
laughing, which did not help, and I still had to read my report
calmly over the air.

I rattled it off, then snapped "Over and out," before the
Isachsen man had time to draw breath.

It took a while to cook supper in the dark but at last it was
ready and as usual tasted delicious. This was the supreme
moment of our existence, to which we had been looking forward
all day. We discussed the problems of travelling in the dark,
over our meal.

"We are the earliest in the field starting from land this far
north, you know," said Roger, an authority on Polar history.

"Peary left on February 27th; Cook too at the end of the month. Plaisted on March 6th and Staib on the 28th. Nansen did start on February 28th but returned to the *Fram* as he came to the conclusion that the cold and dark were too much. He travelled back in an hour and twenty minutes over the distance which had taken him three days struggling hard on the outward leg. He did not set out again until March 14th." Being completely unsupported, we had felt that we needed the extra time, but as I groped and grovelled about I wondered if we were not wasting time living so inefficiently in the dark.

The next day, the 28th of February, it was evident that we were drawing away from the land, in spite of our slow progress. There were more flat areas, with less turmoil. The gently sloping, smooth floes looked as if they had remained unmoving since time immemorial. With only half the load on the sledge we managed to ski. It was bliss, gently coasting over the velvet surface. We were brought to an abrupt halt by a thirty-foot high wall. I scaled it with difficulty and peeped over the top. Utter chaos again—acres of boulders and blocks. "Hopeless," said Hugh. "We will have to back-pack." But suddenly I saw a way through. Directly below us was a smooth path. It wove off to the west but it seemed to me it went back north like a pencil scribble over a page, and I could trace it for a good half mile. We dropped everything down into my Grand Canyon, which was perhaps three feet wide. The sheer walls towered up without a break. I had a feeling of claustrophobia as we eased the sledge round a bend with a third of the load aboard.

"Supposing we meet a bear, head on?" said Roger as the canyon became narrower and narrower. The walls were now pure blue as if they should be lying fathoms deep in the sea. Some corners were so sharp that we had to unload the sledge, haul it up into a perpendicular position then lay it down and reload it round the bend.

After a while my route turned to the south, and, rather thankfully, I agreed that we must climb out. Scaling the walls we clambered up on to a raised floe. It was covered with deep soft powdered snow. We were up to our thighs in it before we realised. Floundering about, we hauled up the boxes and lost them as they sank below the surface. There was a feeling of altitude, and the scene was as if one had made an early start in the high Alps. The snow crystals were actually glinting in the moonlight. It was fantastically beautiful.

But to make progress was a heartbreak. I heaved one leg out, lifted it forward, threw my weight on it in order to extract the other. I lost my balance and actually disappeared under the snow. I fought my way up for air and wallowed on. Far from riding on the surface the sledge sank as much as us and ski-ing was as impossible. I fell again. This time I felt my legs flailing in air. "Crevasse," I shouted. "Quick, quick, haul me up." Hugh caught my wrist and pulled, but one foot was trapped by a hard ice ledge. He pulled harder and my boot and duffel socks came off! Quickly Roger dug and rescued them before they disappeared for good. A few minutes of standing barefooted in the snow at temperature of minus 56 degrees Fahrenheit had frozen them solid. My leg felt wooden as I thrust it back into the boot. "Don't want to linger in these temperatures," said Roger. And he was only too right.

I was at my gloomiest that night in the tent. It was now minus 58 degrees Fahrenheit, and felt like it. We had spent all day struggling hard and had moved perhaps three-quarters of a mile. I felt cold right to my core. The sleeping-bag was sodden, so we thrust it over the rope in the apex of the tent, letting it dangle down, occupying the little space available. The wet fabric slapped me in the face like a floppy haddock every time I moved. The finer points of living were quite forgotten as we huddled in an area a fraction of that of a space capsule. Hugh was low too. He had realised that we had used up three gallons of paraffin in eight days and we would have to cut down. The alternative was to run out far short of our goal. Hugh's nose had become frost-bitten that day, and he looked awful as he sat in the corner with the yellowish dead growth in the middle of his face.

"I'll divorce you if your nose falls off," I muttered. Roger laughed, but I was not all that sure if I had meant my remark as a joke.

"St David's day tomorrow," said Roger, cheerfully looking at his almanac. "First of March. We will be seeing the sun soon. I think I will go to the Greek Islands for my holidays." I longed for a jungle full of growing, green things, and heat. Hugh doesn't go in for holidays in the normal way. All he could talk about was an expedition with the children—a dog-sledge journey across Ellesmere Island to Greenland, perhaps with some Eskimo hunters. I said I had had enough of the North and had no intention of ever coming here again.

Roger was right, there was a pinkness in the sky the next day and in holiday mood we stopped for lunch. It was a change actually to see what we were eating. For the first time I noticed our lack of washing up. The snow that day was glorious—a skier's dream if only it were not so cold and we did not have so far to go. I prepared tomato soup and toasted biscuits. I slipped my slab of butter into my bra to thaw. The boys insisted that I did the same with theirs.

Nothing stopped us that day. We wended our way over small short floes and across numerous leads. We found a gap in the pressure ridges. In spite of this it was impossible for us to travel very far when we still had to go back for the next load. Also in this temperature we found it absolutely impossible to stay outside for more than six or seven hours without the cold boring into one, creeping up from one's feet until one stood, arms stiff, quite unable to move.

March 3rd was the same as usual until at 11 a.m. I glanced back over my shoulder. Suddenly I saw the sun! It was peeping over the hills behind Mount Walker, an orange, pale half orb. It had an extraordinary effect on me. I felt mad with excitement. I remembered a poem in Nansen's book:

> "For the sons of men,
>   Fire is the best
>   And the sight of the sun."

Suddenly I felt for the first time that I really could reach the Pole. Of course we could push on! Of course we could cover the distance! Of course we would get there! We decided to celebrate with a brew-up of tea. We pitched the tent and were soon inside, in a jubilant mood, effervescing with enthusiasm. The manic phase lasted an hour or two until we realised that we must get back to work.

We were pulling through soft snow for four hours and made exactly half a mile. But the scenery was opening out—the floes were larger and the pressure ridges much farther apart. A wind was getting up which froze my breath, joining my hair to my nose and chin. I felt like a West Highland white terrier, quite unable to see. The boys' hairy faces were constantly white with hoar frost and I must have looked just as peculiar. Each day the sun pushed higher and higher and showed more of its face above the British Empire Range, as the mountains of North Ellesmere are called. It looked like a child's sun—a yellow ball. It seemed to have an extra dimension and even texture. There was no heat yet, but the sight of it brought life back to our dead world.

It made me conscious that there was another world, less cold and hostile. I hoped my children were playing outside. I thought of my little fat Rory most, his baby smile a joy to see. I felt as far from Hugh as from my children. He had switched on his expedition wavelength and I no longer felt we were husband and wife. A veil had fallen between us, and even snuggled in our sleeping-bag I felt conscious of the gulf.

Bad weather followed the return of the sun and during the days of early March we became used to a constant biting wind and poor visibility. One morning was worse than usual. The fabric of the tent flapped ominously above the roar of the Primus. I pulled the draw-strings of my inner hood tight so that only my eyes and nose were exposed. I made sure that the warm fur flap round my outer hood was extended, then reluctantly crawled out of the tent.

The wind battered at me, tearing at my clothes. Drifting snow obliterated everything. I could only just make out the sledge five feet away. But our trek to the north was now a race with time calling for every ounce of effort. There was no question of a lie-up day. We just had to go on. Pitting oneself against the elements in these latitudes demands one's utmost and unless one is prepared to give it, one should stay off the polar pack.

The wind came from the north-east, gusting across the ice and curling the loose snow into a dense cloud of moving fury as we struggled to dismantle the tent. Stiff with ice, we had to stamp it flat before rolling it up and then force it into the nylon bag. "Character building," said Hugh, as a bundle fell off the sledge for the umpteenth time before Roger could get it securely under the rope. The wind whipped the loose strands into my face as I tried to balance the tent and Hugh put his knee against the load in order to pull the lashings tight. Ice axes and rifle were pushed through the loops on top to be easily grabbed in case of emergency. By the time everything was stowed and packed the wind had obliterated all traces of our overnight stop.

I set my face against the driving snow. In the front, I was out of contact with Hugh and Roger. I might have been completely alone. I held the compass, useless though it was in this latitude, in my left hand. Without its needle we had absolutely no idea of which way to go. The magnetic variation was about ninety-four degrees as the magnetic pole now lay about 700 miles to the south. I set off into the opaque wall of moving snow. I had a strange feeling I was walking along a path with a high hedge on either side. It was like groping in the dark. Every now and then a mound of pressure ice would loom up like a menacing giant. Time and time again I fell right over a ridge of drifted, hard-packed, wind-blown snow. This sastrugi, as it is called, halted the runners of the sledge. Hugh then had to lift up the front of the sledge and Roger and I would brace our shoulders for an extra heave. "Two, four, six," would shout Hugh and we would all pull at once. The cruel wind brought tears to my eyes which would instantly freeze. The cold struck me to the marrow. The lack of visibility muffled the limitless world giving me a secret place to retreat. What a slim hold on life we had out here, I reflected. One shrug of the spirit that governs the polar pack and we would be dead. It was so cold. I cringed inside my body, but Scott's last entry in his diary came into my numbed mind. "We took risks, we knew we took them. Things have come out against us, and therefore we have no cause for complaint." Fair enough, it was our decision to come, knowing full well the conditions we were going to meet. It was no use complaining now.

I had to force myself to think of something to think about as I inched forward into the wind. Otherwise I would go mad. The utter desolation of the scene was overwhelming. I withdrew from it and concentrated on trivialities. I reorganised my garden with a bed of chrysanthemums in the middle and replanned the nursery for my three boys at home. I cut off from the hell of a world around me by reliving times in the past. I remembered walks in the woods in spring, the buds and snow-drops and the song of a chaffinch. I thought of climbs in Glen-coe in the sun. The rocks warmed my finger-tips as I felt for a hold. I was not meant for polar regions, I reflected, the moun-tain tops were far nearer to my heart. A polar traveller has to be patient, with an inner strength that will keep him plodding on and on. He has to know that there is a destination at the other end of this snow and ice. I need a summit to see that I can aim for and marks of progress to spur me on. Here one would travel 200 miles and be no nearer to one's end. Strange there have been no women polar explorers, I thought. Yet it is mental strength one needed here, not muscle and brawn. Hugh con-sidered one woman an asset on an expedition but any more, he said, were intolerable, causing trouble and unrest. His opinion is that men put up with each other's deficiencies and like each other in spite of the snores and grinding of teeth that get on one's nerves when home is a tent. Women on the other hand try to "improve" their companions and fight a situation rather than fitting themselves in. Vocally, of course, I disagreed, but I had my doubts that an all women's expedition to the Pole could succeed. Some day, I mused, I would lead one and see. All that came to my mind were trivialities. Deep philosophy does not go with physical effort. I have discovered I need to lie on a beach in the sun before my brain will work on a higher plane.

Time passed. I became intolerably hungry. The cold eats up one's resources, and now we had been going for more than four hours. In my pockets were two bars of chocolate and I longed for them. But the difficulties involved seemed insurmountable. I could not face bending my arms, hanging stiffly by my side, and so stirring up the blood. I could never remove my gloves. My fingers would find it impossible to open the paper and how could I ever get a piece into my mouth? So much for the chocolate. I felt as if it was absolutely out of reach.

The texture under my feet suddenly changed. Peering into the swirling snow, I realised we had reached a frozen lead stretching into the nothingness in front of us and I felt that it extended just as far to either side. Was this Peary's "big lead" at last, I thought. He had come across areas of open water at approximately the same latitude on his three attempts on the Pole and he regarded this as a permanent feature of the pack. It was unfrozen when he met it in 1906: twelve miles or so of open water lying between him and the next floe. "We had better go back and fetch the rest of the load now in case the wind opens the lead and separates the floe," yelled Hugh above the blasting of the gale. The ice of the polar pack lies on the surface of the Arctic Ocean rather like a film of dust on a bucket. The wind and the currents in the water move it about causing leads to open in one place and close in another. Winds such as we were having could set a vast area of ice into motion. We must on no account be separated from part of our load.

It was marvellous to turn my back on the gale and dump part of our luggage. Following our tracks was already difficult but without a load on the sledge we could move fast enough to keep warm. Even so there are limits to the length of time one can stand exposure in these conditions before one's temperature begins to fall. We were breathing in air at minus 56 degrees Fahrenheit that day, which the lungs had to warm up to 98 degrees before the oxygen in it was acceptable to the blood. Much latent energy is expended in this process and the body becomes very tired. Also one pants for breath as if short of air, which only makes the situation worse.

Back we trekked to the brink of the big lead. Then for the first time since leaving Weldy's plane we loaded everything on the sledge as one load. Incredulously we found that it would move. It was frightening launching off on to the smooth ice when we had no idea whether it extended for one mile or more. Supposing there was open water in the middle, supposing the ice cracked as we began to move! The drifting snow masked my feet, giving the illusion of trying to make headway on an escalator that's going in a wrong direction. I was torn between the delight of easy going and tiredness that made me curse the

lead for lasting so long, and yet it was easier to continue than to
stop to battle with the tent.

Hugh called a halt at 7 p.m.—our longest day. We mustered
the last sparks of energy and soon the camp was set. Hugh
crawled into the tent and I listened expectantly for the Primus
to burst into life. Nothing happened. Only curses issued from
inside. The stove refused to light. Hugh tried again. He
fumbled in the dim light with a spanner to change the burner.
No good. He unscrewed it and replaced the first one complaining loudly at Roger's spare parts, bought in the little back shop
in Dumfries. Hugh is an expert on Primuses so I did not begin
to worry yet. But heat equals life in these latitudes and I was
shivering with cold.

"You will have to put in a new nipple," said Hugh to me as I
huddled over him. "My fingers are too big." Reluctantly I took
off my gloves. My hands worked like amputated stumps as I
fiddled with the tiny piece of brass. I just had to find the threads
and screw it into place. I dropped it and it vanished on the tent
floor. We had another one though and I tried again. It was
something which really had to be done now. My shivers had
stopped. After the fourth try I managed to get it in and sat back
while Hugh poured the alcohol over the burner and struck the
match. Nothing doing, it still wouldn't go. The grimness of the
situation made me weep. But Hugh is always a one to try again.
Yet another idea—"Give me something to filter the paraffin
with," he called to Roger who willingly tore a piece off the
bottom of his shirt. We had anticipated difficulty with paraffin
at such very low temperatures and so had imported the most
highly refined, but water is always present in this fluid and the
cold causes ice crystals to form which block the Primus burner
tube. Sure enough, as Hugh filtered it through the material, a
slushy mess remained. He filtered it carefully three times before
refilling the stove and tried yet again. "Oh, God," I prayed.
Still it wouldn't go. We were beginning to edge our way into
the frozen folds of the sleeping-bag. Suddenly the stove spurted
and spluttered and a flame appeared on the burner—then
began to grow. Life was worth living again.

The agony of thawing one's fingers is quite different from
anything that I have experienced. First an excruciating pain,

which subsides into a dull toothache, and then fantastically one goes into an ecstasy as one realises that at any moment one will be warm.

Neither Nansen nor Scott used a stove to heat the tent, which enabled both to carry only a fraction of the fuel which we considered essential. Nansen cooked over an ingenious stove of his own invention. It consisted of two silver boilers enclosing a paraffin lamp while a vessel for melting snow sat on top. The hot air could not escape until it had passed round the boilers and under the top can and was then forced down by an aluminium lid to the bottom of the apparatus. Nansen claimed that 93 per cent of the heat yielded by the lamp was utilised for cooking and was proud of how little was wasted to heat the air in the tent. He and his companion Johannsen lay shivering in the sleeping-bag while they waited for their meal to cook. When it was ready, they spread a blanket between them as a table cloth and ate up their pemmican. "I thought it wonderfully comforting," wrote Nansen later. "It seemed to warm us to the very ends of our toes."

Warm now, like Nansen, I slept the sleep of the just. The morning brought a strange silence. There was no wind. The sun was actually sparkling on the snow and I felt I could see heat if not actually feel it. There was less soft snow now. The surface of the floe was quite different, granulated as if seared by wind and polished as if by sand-paper. The hummocks of pressure ice were rounded off by time and drifting snow, and we passed little ponds of clear green ice. "Last summer's melt," explained Roger. But I could not credit that anything would ever thaw here. The scene changed with every step. One stretch of pack ice was totally different from the next. The sledge made a high-pitched rumbling noise as the runners ground over the surface and the squeak of the skis on the snow made it impossible for me to hear the others speak. But apart from us nothing moved. "Where no birds sing" came often to my mind.

We camped in the middle of a large old floe the night after the wind. Bed was as delectable as ever and we were soon asleep. At 3 a.m. I heard a rumble as if a tank were approaching, then utter silence. I put my head down again. But lying in the sleeping-bag I suddenly felt the ice below actually trembling—

then there was a thundering, terrifying roar and a rush as of a hurricane. The ice shook with the noise. The three of us shot up. We kicked our way out of the sleeping-bag and fumbled for boots. Mine were so frozen, I could not get them on. I thrashed my way out of the tent after the others with my feet only half in the boots. We stood up outside the tent. By the light of the moon I could see a dark line stretching right across the floe. I took a moment or two to comprehend. Our floe had split in two! Roger and Hugh were frantically jerking out the ice axes which held the tent. "For God's sake hurry up," yelled Hugh at me. "Can't you see the cracks?"

A thin black line zigzagged about me as if a giant hand had dropped a cheap white plate. The boys pulled the tent bodily back towards some old round hummocks. What's the good, I thought, where can we go? A fatalistic feeling had crept over me. I could not resist going gingerly forward. Two steps brought me to the brink. A gap of three feet lay between me and the rest of our floe. The edges were absolutely sheer, dead straight. I could not believe that the ocean lay between. I bent down and touched it. It felt warm. There was an air of complete tranquillity about. The lines "Still the night, Holy the night," came to my mind. What force had shattered this floe, thirty feet thick at least and three or four miles wide?

The water was a dark navy-blue. Little chunks of white ice were floating placidly in it, like ducks on a pond. I joined the others—piling our belongings on the sledge and pulling it over to the tent. By a stroke of luck we had lost nothing. We scrambled back into the tent and struggled into the sleeping-bag. Already it was crinkling with ice. From a warm haven it had turned into a freezing pit. We lay shivering and listened to the ice rumbling like distant artillery and wondered if our floe would break again.

How near death were we? I considered, as I huddled against Hugh. My mind turned to my dead brother, who I had not thought about for months. He had been killed by Arab terrorists in Muscat, three years before.

"It is odd how family feeling is stirred by anything that makes one feel the universe one's enemy," said Bertrand Russell. How right he was. I thought of others who had died on the polar pack. What about Hall? He was the leader of the Smithsonian expedition, of 1871, that had set out to reach the Pole. He had left his ship, the *Polaris*, and made a sledge journey to about 500 miles from the pole. He retraced his steps, but once back on the ship, he fell ill, and, as he grew weaker, he insisted that he had been poisoned! Hall died, and a Naval court of inquiry was set up, but concluded that he had died from "natural causes". However, a few weeks before we had set out for Resolute, I had been browsing through some copies of the American *Newsweek*, and, to my astonishment, had come on an article stating that Hall had indeed been poisoned, by arsenic!

Two Americans, a Dr Loomis and a Dr Paddock had ferreted out Hall's grave in North Greenland, at "Thank God" harbour, and dug sixteen inches down to uncover a white pine coffin, buried in loose shale. They prised off the lid, and found Hall's body, wrapped in the American flag. The detectives then gazed at the body, well preserved by the cold, as if in fact it had been deposited in one of the Americans grisly refrigerated mortuaries of today, where one buys space to lie in the cold till Kingdom come. However, Loomis and Paddock now removed some fingernails and pulled out some hair, and hastily repaired south to their air-conditioned laboratories. Neutron-activation analysis was used to test the samples. In this process a specimen is placed in a nuclear reactor and irradiated so that any chemical elements present will be transformed into radio-active isotopes. When poor Hall's fingernails were treated, they showed that he had eaten very high doses of arsenic over a two week period before his death!

Why? Hall had been a hard-driving lone wolf, and on a previous expedition had killed a man for threatening mutiny. He had disliked the German doctor that he had with him at "Thank God", and also quarrelled with his second-in-command, a whaling captain called Sydney Budington. Both these men wanted Hall to bale out and retreat south, rather than winter where they were. No one is any the wiser as to what happened, but the rest of Hall's party were well punished for any guilty consciences, as they met disaster after disaster before reaching home.

In the morning the rift was completely solid and it was difficult to register that anything had happened to disturb our night's sleep. There was a delicate violet tinge in the sky to the south. It was the same wan sky that one sees over southern marshes, fringing into purple and blue. Bad weather somewhere, I thought. Perhaps that had caused the movements under our floe. This was our twenty-first day on the ice. Roger reckoned that the sun was still too low for a sextant reading, so we were not quite sure of our distance from the land.

Navigation on the polar pack is similar to that of a small boat, with some fundamental and very important differences. Before radio, the navigator relied exclusively on the position of the sun, moon and stars. Provided he knew the time accurately it was possible for him to fix his position by measuring the angle between himself and the heavenly body by means of a sextant. Because of the rotation of the earth all heavenly bodies appear to move across the sky during a period of twenty-four hours. Therefore the angle to them varies depending on the time of day that the sextant reading is taken.

But there are some special problems with navigating on the polar pack. Perpetual daylight, caused by the sun in the sky for twenty-four hours, makes it impossible to use star shots as in marine navigation and the moon is seldom available. The nearer any heavenly body is to the earth's horizon, the greater refraction there is likely to be. The light from all stars and planets is refracted or bent as it passes through progressively thicker layers of the earth's atmosphere. This means that no star is exactly in the position it appears to be. Normally a correction is made for this.

However, at points below about fifteen degrees above the horizon refraction is greatly increased and in the polar regions where there is frequent ice-crystal precipitation, this refraction can sometimes produce a situation where the sun can appear to be as much as twenty degrees higher than it really is. Since the sun is always low on the horizon, with a maximum height at the north pole on midsummer's day of no more than twenty-three degrees, refraction is always something which must be taken into consideration. But the polar traveller has also to contend with the frozen sea. The marine navigator measures

the angles of a body above the horizon. For accuracy the horizon should normally be at least three or five miles from the
observer. But the polar pack is not flat. It is criss-crossed with
pressure ridges up to thirty feet high and it is often not possible
to see five miles ahead in any direction whatsoever. Since finding a normal horizon is useless, the sextant must have an artificial horizon attached to it. This consists of a little container of
alcohol with a bubble in the middle. The heavenly body is
viewed through the alcohol and the sextant must be held so
that it appears in the centre of the bubble. The angle on the
sextant is then read. This method is both more difficult and less
accurate than on a normal sextant, the main problem being to
hold the bubble steady. But the great difficulty that one is up
against in the polar pack is the cold. It affects all instruments.
The oil in the chronometer freezes and the clock stops; the
alcohol becomes sluggish and the bubble useless. Roger also
found it extremely difficult to use his sextant with gloves. Both
Nansen and Peary had trouble with their chronometers in the
cold and Roger found his affected too. Nansen read his farthest
north as 86°14′. But he probably got farther north than that.
He was particularly careful with sights and refraction and was
always worried that he might be accused with his fixing of his
farthest north. For the final readings he selected the angle which
made him nearer the equator, that is the farthest from the Pole.
Peary, on the other hand, was not so worried. He took only
midday sights. This meant watching the sun for a while round
midday and then taking a series of angles. The highest one is
the midday position of the sun. From this it is easy to find latitude. This is the simplest way to take a sight. But it does not,
however, give one a longitude and so does not take drifting into
account. Near the pole this can be as much as eight miles a day.
Because of this, doubt has been cast as to where exactly Peary
was when he claimed to have reached the Pole. The geographical North Pole is the northernmost point on the earth. All
lines of longitude meet there and it is a definite location. But it
is no particular point on the sea ice (which is in constant movement) and so no fixture is possible as at the South Pole.

Then one has the confusion of the north magnetic pole. This
is the point towards which the compass needle points. It is

moving slowly but surely. At the present moment it is on the
southern tip of Bathurst Island. But when first discovered by
Ross in 1831, it was on the end of Boothia Peninsula. The
compass has a horizontal and vertical component and usually
only the horizontal needs to be taken into consideration. However, at a distance of less than 500 miles from the magnetic
pole the vertical pull on the compass needle is such that the
horizontal swing is seriously affected. The needle becomes
sluggish and unreliable. Close to the pole in fact it is completely
useless. But tables have been drawn up and we knew by referring to Roger's nautical almanac that for the moment and for
the next hundred miles or so we could use the compass provided
we took the error into consideration. We had, however, another
aid to navigation. The wind blew so constantly from east or
west that the lines of wind-blown snow always appeared to lie
at right angles to our direction. Provided we crossed them in
this position, we would be heading north.

On we pushed over easy going floes until forced to stop by
yet another wall. I scrambled to the top, then, horrified, I
beckoned the others to come and look. Below us was a whirl-
pool of ice. It was frozen but only just—a petrified Corri-
vrechen, as if some playful giant had paused in a game.
Smooth floes the size of tennis courts and twenty feet thick had
been tipped like a pack of cards. Huge bridges of ice as large as
a suburban bungalow had been crushed like sugar lumps.
Forty-foot pillars of ice were tumbled on their sides. There was
no level area even on which to stand. This turmoil must have
happened recently. The ice was still green.

We separated for a reconnaissance. I went off to the east.
Forced to detour more and more to the right, I began to
despair. Then I noticed a ramp along the brink of an upturned
floe. This led to another and another. I had discovered the
key! I rushed back to the others waving my arms with excitement. Roger misread my movements and slipped out the
bear gun! My route was aerial and acrobatic but eventually
we were round—similar to the Pilgrim's Progress, I thought.
Out of the Valley of Despair only to meet another more
formidable foe.

There was a mistiness to our left now. "It's like the battlefields of France," said Roger. "Gas creeping over the Somme."

"It's open water," said Hugh ominously. "That's hoar frost smoke," he explained. "It was formed by cold air over warm water." A pressure ridge bent in our direction with a cleft over which the mist was hovering. It looked ghostly and evil like a scene from a film by Ingmar Bergman shot in the forests of Sweden.

I pressed on and tried to ignore the mist approaching slowly and relentlessly from the left. The edge of a lead drew me up. It was half a mile wide and half of it was of a brown chocolate colour—the sign we now knew of only a recent freeze. I prodded it with my axe. "It seems all right," I said to Hugh. He tried a thrust, and water welled up round the shaft. "Impossible here," he said. But slightly to the east the new ice had rafted with slabs of wafer-thin brash piled on top of each other, signifying that floes on either side were coming together. We decided to risk a crossing here. We pulled the sledge to the edge of the slightly thicker ice and then I held my breath—and prayed—and stepped hurriedly on to it. The boys followed and then the sledge. I moved as fast as possible over what was by no means solid ice. I quickened my pace but my rope felt taut. I looked round to see Hugh chatting to Roger about cooking seals! I cursed him. "For heaven's sake hurry up," I said. I noticed an ominous blue-black crack running right across my path. The ice was buckled now so I pushed on at high speed. There's no room for ditheryness here, I thought. But the buckled ice, I suddenly realised to my horror, was flattening out and the water was creeping up. The insidious mist was hovering closer and closer. The dark line was widening. Glancing over my shoulder I saw that the mist now encircled us and there was as much of it to our right as to our left. It was a trap! We were cut off. I saw a place where I thought I could jump and pulled the sledge towards it. "That's no good," warned Hugh. "The landing is on two-inch thick ice. See how it is hinged." Hurriedly we withdrew. Hugh now took over the lead and led us a few yards to the east. "Give me some slack," he shouted back and took a flying leap into the air. I just could not bear to see whether he landed on the floe or not. He was all right. "Quick, quick," he shouted. "Jump!" But I knew that it was far too wide for me. "Go on," yelled Roger from behind us. "It's now or never." There was nothing for it. I closed my eyes and jumped. I got over and far farther than necessary, too. I looked back. The shelf that Roger and the sledge were still on was swaying and sagging from the weight. Roger pushed the sledge from behind, Hugh and I hauled on the rope. We got it over with only the back few feet of the runners getting wet. I did not dare stop to draw breath. There were more widening cracks in front of us. We seemed unable to hurry from this evil place. A line of pressure ice lay ahead at least forty feet high and it seemed to me the most desirable haven in the world. Now there was an extraordinary noise like steam under pressure in a laundry. We might as well be on a volcano, I thought. The squeakings and gasps grew louder and louder. All round us the ice was churning with activity. The wind had gone down and I felt as if the world was lost and, chilled to the bone with shock and worry, I glanced at Hugh for support. Heavens, I thought, he's actually enjoying it. With a smile on his face he was jumping from floe to floe.

"It's the Ides of March, you know," said Roger. "Something was bound to happen today." Never had the sledge travelled so fast. I pulled and heaved with all my might and fairly ran over the first few yards of floe. Roger, in jocular mood said, "At least we won't be killed on the roads this Easter. Think of all the people who will." We camped that night on top of a large uncomfortable chunk of ice.

"Radio sked day," announced Hugh, and he set about the long cold task of spreading out the antenna, heating the generator, tuning the radio. I composed the message for the *Telegraph*, spelling it out, fumbling with cold fingers. Four hours later we were ready to begin.

"Simpson mobile, Simpson mobile calling JAWS." Our call was picked up instantly.

"Simpson mobile, this is Alert—have you anything important to say? We are busy."

"No, no, nothing really important," stammered Hugh, put off his mark.

"Okay, okay, over and out." Silence. We looked at each other. Four hours' work down the drain.

"Oh, well," said Hugh. "Try again tomorrow."

Furious with frustration I turned on him. "You idiot, of course it was important," I screamed with rage.

"Don't be unreasonable," said easy-going Roger. "Perhaps he was swigging a Coke. But I would have liked a time check. The chronometer is buggered up. The cold seems to have gone for it too. I've made a discovery," he added, "the gun only fires when there is no bullet up the spout." Roger's grin subdued my wrath.

We took up our territorial rights as usual with Hugh in the back of the tent, me in the middle and Roger at the door. The weight of the drying sleeping-bag lay on my head and shoulders. Conditions were good, I suppose, compared to the men of the whaling days or the Middle Ages. However did they survive streaming walls, icy cold and poor food? I felt tired that night and was soon fast asleep. I woke up in a horror. A polar bear was breathing heavily through the fabric of the tent. I sat up, then realised my mistake. It was Hugh snoring lying flat on his back. I woke him up and rudely told him to turn over. "What an unbearable situation," he said cracking his usual type joke. Then we heard the sound as of wind in a barley field. I felt it pass beneath me. Was it a wave?

The next day we tried another radio sked. The generator was slow to start but Hugh, with infinite patience, coaxed it into life. Suddenly the outside world fluttered into the tent. Snippets of staccato chatter and fast morse keying made me remember Baron Munchausen, the seventeenth-century traveller who came back with horrific tales of his journeys in the North. He had found a place where it was so cold that one's words froze and had to be thawed out later over the fire in order to hear conversations.

"Are you okay?" came the voice of the met. observer out of our radio. "We've had the most unexpected storm. Really bad. Gale force winds. Look out for heavy ice activity."

Plaisted was held up at about this latitude by bad weather on his first attempt at the Pole. He described the thunder of the tent walls, the roar of the wind, the sibilant rush of the drifting snow becoming a deafening, frightening cacophony. He felt their tents a flimsy barrier against extinction. He imagined a giant outside, wrenching and tearing the tent in his hands, trying to find a way to enter. Plaisted realised that he had now stopped thinking about taking his expedition to the Pole. He was thinking only about keeping the five of them alive. The goal that had dominated his life had been blown away in the wind.

It was the wind that got Scott in the end, too. For four days he and the others lay huddled in their bags, listening to the blizzard. It wore them down, battered at their senses until they were too exhausted to battle with it, too weary to force themselves out and take down the tent, to repack the sledge and lash on the skis and face it all again.

However, blue sky and sun welcomed us out of the tent on March 20th. "It's the equinox," said Roger. "I always recognised in all my calculations that the expedition would do nothing very much before this day of equal light and dark." From now on we would really get cracking.

We encountered low rolling floes like the Russian steppes for the first few hours as we wended our way through newly-stacked piles of pressure ice. The loneliness of a long distance runner was nothing compared to that of a manhauler, I thought as I skied on in front. M'Clintock was the first person who really used this method of travel effectively, and not all that far from here. His was the expedition that went out for Lady Franklin, to search for her husband, who had disappeared with 129 officers and men while looking for the North-West Passage. The irony of the Franklin disaster was that his expedition was the best equipped ever to set out from the shores of Britain. The *Erebus* and *Terror* were manned entirely by volunteers and they had the benefit of a brand new invention—tinned food. It was M'Clintock's great success with manhauling that led Scott to use this method of travel rather than husky dogs, like Amundsen. Another great enthusiast for pulling the sledge himself was Cherry-Garrard. He claimed that his epic trip was "the worst journey in the world". He, Dr Wilson and Lieut. Bowers left in the winter of 1911 to collect the eggs of the emperor penguin which breeds in midwinter. They manhauled to a colony at Cape Royds. They had a terrible journey, being forced to triple relays with temperatures in the minus seventies. The roof of their tent blew away on Wilson's birthday, and they faced one disaster after another. They collected the eggs, however, and finally turned back, just in time. The surfaces were chaotic and the friction made it practically impossible for them to move their sledge. Wet, frozen sleeping-bags and no tent meant little sleep. Cherry-Garrard said they were so tired that their eyes used to close on the march. They manhauled about one hundred miles and arrived back so encased in ice that their clothes had to be cut off.

Looking ahead for a landmark to fix our route, my attention was caught by a particularly large block of ice on the horizon. Was it real, or was it just a mirage? We had been fooled by this type of thing before. But the large block of ice we were heading for turned out to be no mirage.

"It's a berg," said Hugh. "Look at the size of it. Look at the havoc it has caused!"

Ice was piled up thirty feet or so like a slag heap behind, and surrounded it on two sides. There was an area of mangled and shattered floe all round. Between us and the berg was a lead two hundred yards wide. There was a skin of ice on top but it had only just solidified. When we drew to a halt I suddenly heard the noise that the creaking of the sledge had masked until now. Squeaks, gasps and groans. The berg was trying to get free!

It was a calm, clear sunny day and I felt it incredible to credit the forces at work beneath our feet. It would have been a berg like this, I mused, that the *Titanic* had hit on the cold still night in April 1912. The great steel hull of the luxury liner was cut in two with the impact and she upended and slid beneath the sea. One thousand five hundred people went down with the ship, the band playing "Nearer my God to Thee" as the water swept over the deck. I watched the berg, mesmerised by its movements as it wriggled in its grip of ice. There was seven-eighths more of it below the surface I realised with trepidation. The lead stretched to left and right, widening out into a vast area of open water. We walked up and down but I could see at a glance that there was no other way across.

"Let's give it a try," I urged and reluctantly the boys agreed.

We hitched on to the sledge and I strode out on to the black ice. Most exquisite hoar frost crystal formations were still growing on its surface. Pincushions of needle-sharp particles of ice, shaped into petals and leaves. Fixing my eyes on the far side, I set off at high speed. I was a third of the way across before I felt the movement under my feet. I looked back. Horrified, I saw the ice swaying in rhythmical waves which passed beneath me and bounced against the far side before rippling back once more. "Too risky," yelled Hugh, and I was only too ready to agree. Closing my eyes, I hurried back over the swaying ice and we were soon standing disconsolately on the wrong side. "Have to sleep on it," said Hugh. "But heaven help us if the berg escapes in the night."

"Take a look at my feet, Hugh," said Roger hauling off his boots and felt inners. He winced with pain as he removed his socks and a pong of decay wafted in my direction. "I got them wet the other day, and the boots have rubbed a sore. They are a trifle small for me. Remember I was to get another pair?"

One glance told me that Roger had frost-bite. His big toe was swollen—bloated like an uncooked pork sausage. Peary cut off eight of his toes himself on his 1902 expedition, I remembered. The Eskimo treatment is to bite off the toe at the joints and so prevent the ghosts from entering the body. The saliva closes the wound immediately. Sudlavenik told me in Resolute that he had chopped off his little toe to impress a girl, and that it did not hurt provided the leg was frozen stiff. Freuchen describes being driven so mad by the smell of four frost-bitten toes that he fitted a nail puller over each toe and banged it off with a hammer. "I cannot attempt to describe the physical pain," he wrote, "but there was a spiritual pain too, in discarding a portion of my own body, even a part that would never be of any use to me again."

Roger was unimpressed with my words of comfort. "Nansen never had frost-bite," he said dejectedly, "he was too clued up."

Hugh's high-powered medical practice is always along the same lines. "Do as little as possible. Best of all, do nothing." He encased Roger's foot in Elastoplast and told him to put his socks back on quickly before we passed out from the stink.

MARTIN
SAYS !

I was frightened as I lay in the sleeping-bag. I would have preferred a mad dash rather than just sit tight and listen to the noise of factory works and electrical saws. I prefer valour to discretion, I thought, as the noise of creaking came from under my head. The night was full of noises of machinery and I dreamt of a man with an electrical saw directly underneath the tent.

Hugh woke me up at 3 a.m. and placed a bar of chocolate in my hand. It was our tenth wedding anniversary. The first any couple has spent at 84°N, I thought, as I remembered where we were. "Thanks. I wonder if we will have an eleventh," I said gloomily to Hugh. "Why ever not?" he said, quite unmoved by our situation.

The ice looked steadier and stronger in the morning and we decided to try to cross. At one place it was darker grey. I gingerly stepped on it and it took my weight. I looked back at the crucial moment and found that instead of holding my rope Hugh was fumbling with his camera. "It will be the most valuable photograph of the expedition, if you do fall in," cracked Roger in his deadpan voice. We were now all spread out on the ice. One is not frightened when there is something to do. I concentrated on keeping the rope at my waist taut, and maintaining a straight line. Squeaks and puffs still emanated from the berg as I looked into the green grotto it had eroded for itself in the floe. I had felt until now that the Arctic, like the jungle, was neutral. It was not actively against us, but that berg seemed genuinely evil. Thank heaven that's behind us at last, I thought, as we reached the far side, and I scrambled on to the floe. I was glad to be away from the place. What was in front of us could never be as bad as what now lay behind, I thought, with a new spurt of life. The snow sparkled in the sun now and the sky was blue. The coming of spring, I felt, and I suddenly had a great longing for chestnut buds and greenery. We were crossing an area of big, old, weathered floes with indiscriminate pressure ice dotted about on the surface. Sometimes floes would ride on top of each other and we had to clamber up a wall. But there was nothing to stop our progress. All we needed was time. We still could not go fast because friction gripped the runners of the sledge like a child's sticky fingers in one's hand. No two days were the same. Whiteouts, mist, sun, calm weather or tearing wind. We made the most of the daylight and started to stir at 3 a.m. Life had to be simple when camping under our conditions and we all ate a one-course breakfast. I stirred oats, tea, butter, milk, sugar and apple flakes into our one bowl and we ate up the slushy result with relish. Roger called it "Eskimo tea", and said that on his journey over Smith Sound, Peter Peary had added cocoa as well!

Owing to our nutritional research, every twelve days we were changing our diet from high protein to low. Calories remained the same in both—more butter in one, more meat in the other. High protein days were the best. We were cold and hungry on the low, as now, and felt the need for far more bulk. Breakfast over, Hugh worked at his medical research results, Roger filled in his meteorological notes and I wrote my diary. I was always far too tired to do so in the evening. "March 24," I wrote. "Grim weather. Cold, cheerless; deep soft snow. Little leads. Roger's lip stuck to brass of sextant while taking sight. Hugh prised it off. Tore skin. Into area of solidified turmoil. Water spout or something has thrown up acres of green ice." There was not time for more. Our entire life was geared to pushing on. By 7 a.m. we were on our way, lashing up the sledge then off, over floes, across leads and up the pressure walls. We traversed one particularly old floe that was dotted with fragments of pressure ice that looked like monoliths or ghostly gravestones.

We ate a bar of chocolate for lunch on the move. The weather was certainly getting warmer. I could now bear to take my glove off and remove the paper from the chocolate. The sun completely encircled us and by the time it was due west we were ready to call it a day. We put up the tent, fell into it and struggled to keep awake while supper cooked.

I toyed with my diary. I wished I had followed Scott's practice of writing on one side of the page only. Already mine was nearly illegible. I noticed the date. In a week's time it would be Hugh's birthday. I had left a present for him at Resolute, to come in with the re-supply at the Pole. We'd better hurry up, I thought, if he is going to get it on the appropriate day. It was on his birthday that Oates had said quietly to his companions, "I am going outside, and may be some time." The party was thirty-one miles from One Ton Depot and Oates gave them the opportunity to reach it.

March 26th was a good day until we came to a sharp rift in an old floe at 3.30 p.m. "Have to carry," said Hugh, so we unlashed the sledge. Roger jumped down into the gap, only his yellow hood showing above the brink. I handed down the boxes one by one. Then the bulky loads, the tent bulging with ice, the polystyrene floor and then the sledge.

Hugh lifted the loads out at the far side and set them on the level floe beyond. Nothing left, on my side, of the narrow rift. "Want a hand?" asked Roger as he gave me a push from behind to help me up the almost sheer wall, with no footholds, on the far side. I can still feel the wind in my face as it blew from the north-west, an unusual quarter, that day. I can remember it all with heartbreaking intensity, because it was our last day heading north.

CHAPTER SIX

I LIT THE Primus under the billy-can, melted the snow in it and brought it to the boil. Then I carefully poured it into the rubber bottle and handed it out to Hugh who placed it in the insulated box that housed the generator and lifted the machine on top. Then he firmly replaced the lid. He had been outside tinkering with the blasted generator since 6.30 a.m. It was now 10 a.m. For three hours the previous evening he had battled with it too with no success.

Suddenly Roger and I heard the noise of the generator above the noise of the Primus. I breathed a sigh of relief. Soon we would have the radio sked over and would be on our way. Then a few coughs and a spluttering noise and silence. "What's up?" I queried Hugh. No answer. I pushed open the tent door and looked out. Clouds of smoke! Hugh was bending over the little generator, a look of astonishment and horror on his face. "It went on fire," he said. "Short circuit, I suppose." I stiffened. A chill crept over me. "Let's mend it," I shouted, slightly hysterical already.

Roger dug for the bag of spare parts and the works manual while I fished for the spanners and a screwdriver. Hugh crawled back through the tent door dragging the machine behind him. The bright red case was blackened and the paint blistered. But, really worrying, bubbles of molten plastic were oozing out of the component at one end. Hugh is the ever hopeful mechanic at heart. But I knew, with a sickening intensity, that our generator could not be mended in the field.

Hugh had chosen this particular 300-watt petrol generator because the Plaisted Expedition had successfully used an identical model on their snow-scooter journey to the Pole the previous year. Their generator had survived all the bumps and strains and cold they had encountered and we had expected it to do the same for us. Of Japanese make it had proved itself also on Everest and was used regularly by the Americans in their South Pole base.

But the fact was that our's had let us down. Hugh traced the circuit diagrams and unwound wires on the tent floor. "Perhaps we can make some new insulation for the voltage regulator," he said hopefully. "That appears to be the site of the trouble," he diagnosed in a pathological voice. The hours went by while Hugh checked the soldering points and fuses for the umpteenth time. The sun shone on the tent. I sat at one end stiff and absolutely still. Roger half lay in the middle pretending to read *Martin Chuzzlewit*. Neither of us said the forbidding words that I knew Hugh would ultimately utter.

"We will have to go back."

"Oh, God," was all I could say and I put my head in my hands and wept. Tears welled through my fingers. All the difficulties of the past weeks ran through my mind—the cold, the open water, the dangerous berg, the fighting for miles.

" 'I can face one failure,' Shackleton said," quoted Roger in a broken voice. "He turned back 90 miles from the South Pole."

"Well, I can't!" I shouted at him and Hugh. "We've got to go on. I am going to, anyway."

"It isn't possible," reasoned Hugh. "Without radio contact we will not find the scientists at the Pole. Their station is drifting at eight miles per day. If they come looking for us in their little plane, they will never pick out three small figures in the rough ice. Weldy told me that most adamantly before he left. We have only food and fuel until the first of May. Quite apart from that we would not be allowed to push on into the blue. The search and rescue people would be out—2,000 dollars an hour. Even they would not find us out there. They would not know where on earth to start to look."

In Hugh's mind there was no argument—we had to return. Hugh had said to our newspaper sponsors that we would return towards Hunt Island in the event of radio failure or difficulty. He now insisted that we do just that. Roger agreed that this was our only policy.

"Go back quickly, get a new generator and start again—we could probably get off the ice in a week," he said, hopefully.

I refused. We argued all afternoon and well into the night. I lay awake still sobbing. My entire life had been preparing for this journey. I would never get another chance. I had withstood

Myrtle Simpson and Roger Tufft manhauling on Arctic Ocean—
young ice between floes.

Roger Tufft on pressure ice off Ward Hunt Island with open water
beyond. Mountains of North Ellesmere in the background (N.W.T.
Canada). April, 1969.

Roger Tufft refuelling the stove cf the northernmost building (on land) in the world—the hut on Ward Hunt Island. April, 1969.

Myrtle and Hugh Simpson being picked up by plane after attempting to ski from Ward Hunt Island to Alert (near Cape Columbia, N.W.T. Canada). April, 1969.

the cold and physical effort and I knew that I could reach the Pole. I wanted to for personal justification, I suppose. But also I wanted to carry my little Union Jack there far more than that. Poor old Britain, I thought. No one considers us much these days. But the more I travel the more sure I am that our values are right and I want to bring up my children as British. Small-time nationalism infuriates me—I am all for fewer frontiers, not more. Britain as a whole is important to me and I wanted to place my flag at the Pole to compensate for the empty flagstaffs round the world where now it does not fly.

It was Friday, March 28th, when we started back from 84°42′N. We had been five weeks away . . . thirty-five days out on the ice. The Arctic Ocean had seen many failures.

Perhaps Lieutenant Greely of the U.S. was the worst. In 1881 he was in command of an expedition of twenty-five men, who were to establish a station as far north as possible, as part of the American contribution to the International Geophysical year. He and twenty-five others went north on the S.S. *Proteus*, which left them with enough food for three years. Greely set up his base on the east coast of Ellesmere at Fort Conger, in Lady Frank-lin's Bay. The *Proteus* was to return in two years, but Greely had orders to break camp and set off south under his own steam if the ships did not appear. Depots of food were to be cached for him, but, unknown to Greely, this part of the plan was not carried out. Incompetence, bungling and genuine difficulties with the ice resulted in virtually no food being dumped for his journey south. In the summer of 1883 the *Proteus* was crushed by ice and sank. The crew escaped and sailed home on a rescue ship leaving Greely and his men marooned farther north.

Now, according to plan, Greely started out south, but his party was soon in difficulties. Their equipment was completely inadequate for this journey. No food. No sledge. They struggled on, manhauling a heavy ship's boat, living off lichen, seaweed and soup made from their sealskin clothing. The men had guns, but were hopeless hunters, and time and time again failed to retrieve shot seal, walrus and birds. They holed up for a third winter. They ran out of fuel and could think of no way of quenching their thirst, and their sleeping bags froze to the ground. They had no light, and lived on one-fifth rations. One

D

man was driven to stealing this meagre food, and was shot on Greely's command.

When American rescuers eventually came on the scene, eighteen of the men were dead. One body was found on the beach. Most of the flesh had been eaten. Other bodies also showed signs of cannibalism. A spark of life was only just found in Greely and seven of his party. Two of these were sent to prison on their return for insubordination. Greely survived and was promoted to General, but was so embittered by his failures that he opposed other American explorers who came to him for advice. Harshly criticised by Peary, Greely sought revenge by decrying him publicly when Peary claimed to have bagged the Pole.

Peary himself failed four times. He had first consolidated his thoughts of the Pole in 1887 when he was an obscure naval engineer on a ship bound for Nicaragua. They passed San Salvador, and Peary gazed entranced towards the island, alleged to be Columbus' landfall in the New World. Peary wrote in his diary: "Purple against the yellow sunset, as it was almost 400 years ago when it smiled a welcome to a man whose fame can be equalled only by him who shall one day stand with 360° of latitude beneath his motionless feet and for whom the East and West shall have vanished—the discoverer of the North Pole."

Peary tried for the Pole himself in 1898, leaving the U.S. in a ship, the *Windward*, donated by the English publisher Alfred Harmsworth—later Lord Northcliffe. For the next four years he tried again and again to push north, but got nowhere near his objective. In 1902 he turned back, at 84°17'N. But he returned to try once more. He was a bold, arrogant man but I felt for him when he wrote in his diary: "We were forced to return after only fifteen days on the pack. Has the game been worth the candle, and yet I could not have done otherwise than stick to it. . . . I shall be glad to get away from everything here and yet as I look at the cliffs a feeling akin to homesickness comes over me, but it is for the useful, foolish hopes and dreams with which they have been associated."

His most humiliating failure, he said, was in 1906, when he had been able to travel at no more than half his estimated speed of ten miles a day. At the age of fifty, he said, he could not hope for any further attempts. A whole ship had been built especially for him and he felt he just could not face his backers at home. Perhaps Peary was looking for fame rather more than the Pole, which he claimed to have reached in 1909.

This could never be said of Nansen. Did the North Pole in fact, mean much to Nansen? In his Royal Geographical Society address in London in 1892, he had stated that "It may be possible that the current will not carry us across the Pole. But the principal thing is to explore the unknown polar regions, not to reach exactly that mathematical point on which the axis of our globe has its northern termination." Nansen had plans for going to the South Pole on skis, which he hoped to carry out in about 1900, but various commitments prevented it. Then Amundsen asked him for the use of the *Fram*.

Nansen agreed to this but later said that it was the bitterest moment of his life when his ship sailed south down Oslo fjord in 1911. Nansen was then fifty and he considered himself too old for any further expeditions or attempts towards the North or South Poles. My mind on failures, I thought of Scott. His was the greatest disappointment when, after all that effort and trouble, they found Amundsen's little tent perched at the South Pole. But interestingly enough, his companion Wilson did not even mention the fact that Amundsen had got to the Pole first! To the Doctor, the important thing was just to be there, living in the environment of sky and snow. Wilson considered the Antarctic regions the most beautiful in the world and on his earlier expedition had been known to stand for hours in front of his easel with no gloves, painting the scene in water colour, complaining only when his paints froze.

Worse than Scott's situation and even more of a heartbreak than failing to reach the Pole, was Cook's experience. He himself was convinced that he had arrived at 90°N. But no one believed him. He was called a liar and was completely discredited. He was a lone wolf far out from the "establishment", as represented by Peary. He believed that the best way to succeed against natural forces was not to struggle but to go with them. Neither he, Peary, Nansen nor Scott carried a radio, I thought bitterly. Ours represented the weight of two weeks'

food on the sledge, which was quite enough to give us some
leeway to find the Canadian scientists at the Pole. If we had
never had a radio with us, we would not now be turning
back.

"Quit moaning," said Hugh roughly. "The quicker we get
back the more likely we are to be able to set out once more."
Reluctantly, and not very helpfully, I joined the others in
sorting out food and equipment in order to lighten the sledge.
Our future now lay in moving at high speed. Hugh's worry was
to forestall a search and rescue operation that he was convinced
would be put into effect. He accused me of self-pity and
emotion.

"But one does travel on the polar pack on one's emotions," I
argued. "It's a question of mind over matter." One has to force
oneself over the white horizon. To "want" to achieve a polar
goal is more important than vim and vigour. Shame was what I
felt now, I recognised. I was not beaten by the ice of the polar
pack but the boys were not prepared to gamble their lives along
with mine. One trouble was that Hugh and I were together. If
we did not come back, the children would have no parents
whatsoever.

Nansen's wife had faced this difficulty in her day. Mrs
Nansen launched the *Fram* with champagne and it was then
intended that she should also go on the voyage. However, the
captain, Sverdrup, was against it and the crew agreed with
him. So although Nansen was all for it, she did not go. Nansen
said that in the end he reluctantly agreed with the crew, influenced by the fact that if the ship were lost, and they had to make
a long sledge journey, women would force a slow-down of the
party, and might in fact prevent them ever reaching land, thus
leaving an orphaned daughter. Nansen's wife had accompanied him on his ski-ing and sailing trips in north Europe; she
said that her saddest moment was when Nansen sailed off in the
Fram without her.

Bitterly disappointed, I turned round to face the sun. Now
heading due south it would be in our eyes all day long. Ironi-
cally, it was the most glorious day. The temperature was
minus 23 degrees Fahrenheit, warm and comfortable by our
standards, and there was only a light breeze on our backs. The

lightened sledge stirred readily into life and bounced along behind us as we followed our tracks back along the weathered floe. In no time we reached our previous camp. It looked forlorn with a little pile of litter and a few footmarks in the snow.

Scott retraced his footsteps back as far as the Beardmore Glacier and Shackleton also followed his own on his retreat from the South Pole. Shackleton's bad luck had a parallel with ours, I reflected. His logistics depended on eating the ponies that pulled the sledge. The last one fell down a crevasse on the very day that it was to be killed. It would have provided meat for two weeks. Without it Shackleton felt obliged to turn back, although utterly convinced that he could have made the Pole quite easily, given a chance. Scott and Shackleton were the only two people with the experience to equal ours of being so long on the ice, completely unsupported, manhauling the sledge themselves. But both of them were sledging in the summer. On the South Pole the ice is over land; open water need not be taken into consideration, and so one can travel in the summer months. At that time the temperatures are higher, the difficulties are fewer. The cold we were facing broke the films in the camera, broke the fibres of the material of which our windproofs were made. The intense cold snapped the sights off our rifle, stopped Roger's chronometer, expanded the bubble in the sextant and now, its final effect, the disaster of the generator.

Some expeditions have actually been glad to turn back. To have been halted by a genuine insurmountable barrier would not have been nearly so bad as the frustration I felt at that time. I remembered an old manuscript of the voyage of the Portuguese explorer, Jéronimo Côrte-Real. Of one of the great Portuguese expeditions in the Pacific, Real wrote, "their victailes fayling them—they returned backe agayne with joy."

Back we went and back, easily back. Our big lead was frozen solid. The large iceberg stood static in the sun. That first day we covered three camps in one journey and the following day four. There was not a murmur or a squeak from under the ice. Why did the pack hate us so? I thought. It had been doing everything it could to hold us up on the outward journey. We leapfrogged another camp. My mind boggled now as I tried to think backwards. Instead of thinking of today, I was considering us ten days ago. I tried to imagine each previous camp-site in advance. As we gazed back over the floes, it was impossible to remember that I had been there before. It looked as virginal and untouched as when we had been facing the other direction. "A desert wild and wasted, old as unrecorded time."

Heroics have gone with the passage of time, I thought. One is not allowed to be brave any more. The Elizabethans pushed on regardless. Nobody went out and pulled them back.

I thought of the time we had expended collecting those urine samples for Hugh. Would they be of any value, now that we had not made the Pole? I remembered that Scott had written, "With success all roads will be made easy, with failures even the most brilliant may be neglected."

"For God's sake cheer up," said Hugh, quoting Burns. "The best laid plans of mice and men gang aft agley."

We made a new discovery in the tent that night. Our ration biscuits tasted delicious if toasted over the Primus with a piece of frozen butter sizzling on top. One even did not notice if one burnt one's finger-tips in the effort. As we lay down in the sleeping-bag that night, I had a sudden longing to stuff it full of my four children and hold them in my arms. We had been away for so long now that I could not visualise their faces in my mind's eye. Were Robin's freckles to the left or right of his nose? Which eye was it of Rona's had the slight squint? Bruce's face was hard to focus and Rory was probably quite changed by now. The weather was balmy and calm. The sky was in evidence more now instead of just a murkiness above us. There was colour and light in it and a play of clouds.

On April 3rd, a dark bulk appeared in the distance in front of us. I peered and peered at it all day. The atmosphere cleared towards evening. It was the mountains of the British Empire Range! I stood stock-still and gazed at them expecting the vision to drift away with the mist. For the first time the land looked desirable and I began to want to be off the ice. According to Roger we were now the only people to have camped and manhauled in such low temperatures for so long. Nansen and Amundsen turned back for warmer climes and Scott died.

The sun became redder as the day advanced and in the evening turned into a ball of brilliant fire. Shafts of light were scattered over the glowing sky and the snow around assumed the pale rose of an alpine bloom. It was absolutely beautiful and I felt guilty of intruding on the scene. The world felt pre-Adam and Eve, absolutely pure and free of sin. Jewels glinted about us in the sun, rubies and fiery opals shone out as the light was split into its components by the facets and particles of ice. Chiselled by the wind, the ice formed contours and shapes. The light played around them, giving a texture to the surface and raising the flat ice into 3D.

Little indentations in the snow showed me the way—a piece of broken sastrugi or the slightest mark of the sledge. It was all that was left of our struggles of the weeks before. The tracks led across an old smooth floe that evening. With my head down looking for our old route, I hit on a pressure wall. I do not remember that, I thought, looking about in surprise. Sure enough our tracks were there, but perpendicular to the ground!

The floe had been tossed aside, upended and left stranded, our tracks heading crazily for the sky. The new lead beyond it was frozen and we found the tracks again on the far side. I could not help thinking that our route back was too easy and that the pack ice would not let us go scot free. We passed the windy camp where my wrists had become frost-bitten and we slid past the place where I had set up the frozen waves. After a bit of a slope that I remembered well, I came to a stop, speechless. Before me was a sheer drop and a wide expanse of newly frozen lead. Across it was an area of complete chaos; piles of green new pressure ice churned up as though a vast mincer had gone mad. The activity was obviously recent. We were blasé now about this sort of thing and the squeaks and grinding of ever-active pressure did not worry me any more. I was a veteran of the polar pack now; quite at home in this environment. Unmoved, we pushed through and then on to the thin ice beyond. A little bit out was a black line, like a rope uncoiled on the surface or a giant snake. It was an open crack. I just stepped over and moved on. On the mountains I know exactly where to put my feet, which rocks have the holds, and now I felt as in tune with the polar pack although it had not told us all its secrets yet. There was more lead than floe. Recent patches of open water were mixed with rafted sheets of new ice. The entire area showed signs of recent movement. A mist was creeping up from the south and our world was shrinking with every passing minute. We blundered on, picking our way round fingers of floe and avoiding head-on collisions with the open cracks. Visibility now was practically nil. Which way should we go? I began to despair. I could sense open water ahead, chaotic pressure to one side and drifts of deep, soft snow on the other. There was no sign of the land. The sledge mounted ice blocks and rumbled down ridges of upturned floe. I became tired. It was 10 p.m. and no area looked large enough to hold the tent. Gigantic gasps and groans issued from deep under the thick ice and I felt rather like a water beetle on a pond.

"Let's camp here—it's safe enough," said Hugh convincingly, and I was too exhausted both mentally and physically, to argue.

"I feel seasick," I declared after our meat-bar stew. "The camp site must be swaying."

"Rubbish," denounced Hugh, and we slept the night through.

The following day was Good Friday. We cooked breakfast slowly and significantly—it was our last one.

This was the day that we had estimated we would be off the ice. The land looked a stone's throw away in the clear morning light, Walker Hill so close that I could see the boulders lying on the moraine. It was a calm tranquil morning, incredible to think it was the same world as yesterday. A pressure ridge had built up near the tent and puffs and gasps issued from the ice along the edge of our little floe. Hugh shook the Primus. "There is damn all fuel left either. We'll just have to get off today."

The noise of the pressure became more significant as we packed up. I looked round over my shoulder and actually saw our floe breaking at the edge and the big pieces pushed up into a standing position as if by a ghostly hand. We set off in a hurry, the noise growing in intensity following us from behind. We moved out on to the lead to our right but the sound like an express train was catching us up. Now on either side the ice was tumbling and moving. I glanced back. Frost smoke was puffing up about us.

"The lead must be opening, come on!" I urged. Zigzag lines were forming in front of us like a loose jigsaw puzzle. The ice was flooding in places. The sea was surging up and swishing over the surface. We were swept along now by the activity on top of the ice which was jostling for space. Our route was cut off by black water, but I managed to make a small triangular block of ice. It tilted under my weight. I stepped to another and the first one sank. I was floating, actually sailing with the current. White bubbles of air were bounding up as I peered down, intrigued by the movement. The others followed me as I stepped on over the moving blocks as fast as I could. We all heaved at the sledge. Over one block to the next. The noise became louder and louder but the movement was actually slow. Relentlessly the floes were being pushed to one side by the water. The noise of the hitting and grinding of fracturing floes was awful.

Then suddenly, silence, as if a hidden wave below had passed on. All was peaceful under the bright sun. We looked at each other, incredulous. It was hot today. For the first time on the trip I actually pushed down the hood of my anorak. We were inclined to be lazy after our narrow escape. We followed each other to the top of a large block of pressure. We sat down on the summit of the blue ice looking at the view. The land was close, sure enough, but the lead we were on swung round, and between us and the shore was a cloud of black smoke. From where we were sitting it looked as if the whole pack ice had separated from the land-mass of northern Canada. As far as we could see, to the north and to the south, open water stretched out a mile or two wide. We picked our way over tumbled blocks of ice a half-mile nearer the shore but there was no way over that final belt of water. The land was as unobtainable as ever.

We pitched the tent on the very brink of the open water and then stood in a disconsolate row. We had no food and no paraffin. Our prospects were certainly grim. I thought of Scott and his men dying, eleven miles short of One Ton Depot, where ample food and fuel had been cached. I remembered Aeneas

MacIntosh who laid the depots for Shackleton in his 1914 expedition. Shackleton planned to cross the Antarctic continent and intended to set off from the Weddell Sea, call at the Pole and arrive at the Ross Sea on the far side. However, his ship was crushed in the ice and abandoned. All the crew made a fantastic escape to Elephant Island. Then Shackleton and three companions set out to get help from South Georgia and eventually all were rescued. But meanwhile, not knowing this, Shackleton's depot-laying party set out from the Ross Sea sector to lay the food out on the ice barrier as far as the Beardmore Glacier. They accomplished this, led by MacIntosh, and suffered a terrible return journey. The temperatures were low and scurvy set in. They were all in a state of collapse, and one in fact died. But the rest of the party reached Scott's old hut, about twenty miles from Shackleton's base. Here they spent a week or two recovering. But MacIntosh would not wait. He was a man of action and insisted on crossing the thin bay-ice in order to get to their proper base. He left with a companion and was never seen again. It was believed that the wind changed and the ice carried him out to sea. Accidents on mountains usually happen on the way down the hill when one tends to relax after the difficulties of a stiff climb.

"We ought to go to bed," said Hugh. "It will all be solid in the morning."

The prospect of the frozen, stiff sleeping-bag and no Primus even to melt the ice did not fill me with much enthusiasm. We pulled our hoods well over our heads, made sure our gloves came well over our cuffs then brushed the snow carefully off our boots and wedged our way into the bag. I lay down and shivered and shook. But I woke up at 1 a.m. incredibly warm! The heat of our bodies had unfrozen the bag and the temperature inside had built up. How long can one exist without heat when it's minus 22 degrees Fahrenheit at night, I thought? If collapsed in the snow one could die very quickly in the Scottish hills at two above.

I woke Hugh up. "Go and see if the lead's frozen," I demanded. Reluctantly, and rather surprisingly, he agreed. Getting up is easy when one has one's boots on. In an instant Hugh was out of the tent. He was back just as quickly. He shook his head. "Still open water for as far as I can see." We lay in the bed for an hour or two. It is difficult to decide when to get up if there is nothing for breakfast. I could feel Roger's hands fumbling in his pockets.

"What's up?" I asked.

"Look," he replied. In his hand was a packet of biscuits. "Found it yesterday when I was clearing up." Enthusiastically we gobbled them down, one and a half each.

To prevent the sleeping bag from freezing the following night, in case we needed it yet again, we decided that we must have someone constantly inside. I decided to take my turn first, while the others went off for a walk. I was longing to be alone. However, as soon as their footsteps faded I began to feel lonely and to wish that I had gone too. Our conversation at the start of the trip with Weldy Phipps was uppermost in my mind. He had said that there were huts on Ward Hunt Island and fuel and food. I also thought as I lay there that other people had faced the same situation that we were in now. Nansen, I remembered, had made a great landfall after his attempt on the Pole. He had been away for more than three years and thought that he still had a long and difficult journey ahead, believing himself to be on the unknown islands of Gilliesland.

Could the same thing happen to us, I thought. Would there be somebody waiting for us on Ward Hunt Island. At least we expected to find a radio and generator; we had arranged for these to be left for us in the event of radio failure and we just hoped that the *Telegraph* had put this request into action.

There was still time for us to set out again with a new radio if we made a quick turn around.

I envied Staib, the young Norwegian, and Wally Herbert who had replaced broken equipment by means of an air drop. When Staib decided to bale out from his attempt on the Pole he was lucky enough to step straight on to the drifting American weather station, *Arlis II*. He did not have the bitterness of retracing his footsteps as we had now.

Soon we would have to face the taunts of failure. It was said of Franklin that "what he succeeded in doing was vastly more significant than what he failed to do". His failure to reach his destination was a reflection of contemporary over-optimism

rather than a personal limitation. Would our failure to reach
the Pole be measured against our aim to be self-supporting, and
our accomplishment of returning safely to land after forty-five
days on the polar pack? One thing I knew, there would be no
scenes between my children, as there had been in the Franklin
family, when their daughter Eleanor and her fiancé had
eagerly tried to lay their hands on the family fortune before it
was spent on a search for the lost father. Perhaps there is an
advantage in having no money behind one, after all!

I felt the vibration of the boys' feet before I actually heard
them return. "Open water for miles and miles," said Hugh.
"But it is a glorious day. Come out for a walk." I swopped
places with Roger who had been waiting for a chance for the
last three months to finish reading his book.

There was a soft light and the air was warm to breathe. It did
not catch at one's chest as previously and the pack ice was silent
and peaceful—even friendly. The sun appeared benevolent, the
temperature was plus 1 degree Fahrenheit. On foot, with no
pack to carry and no sledge to pull, it was easy going. It was
quite invigorating to jump from one boulder of ice to the next.
There was no level block of more than three feet in breadth, but
some rounded blocks were as big as houses. One was perched on
a pillar about forty feet high and we scrambled up for the view.
There, across the belt of water was land with Ellesmere Island
forming the skyline behind Mount Walker. It loomed up above
us, as dominating as the Buchaille to Rannoch Moor. We looked
down: fresh black ice was mingling with the darker black of
open water, and it stretched away to the west and to the east,
bounded on one side by a chaotic line of pack ice and on the
other by the smooth, shelving sweep of the ice shelf leading up
to the island itself. There was absolutely no way round. A pall
of smoke hung in the sky, a sign that there was a vast area of
open water.

Over one spot there rested a dense black mist, very strongly
resembling a West Indian rain squall, as it looms over the
distant horizon of the sparkling Caribbean. It was obviously
going to take a long, long time to freeze. As we walked back to
the tent, I remembered a description, in Scott's diary, of the
men sitting round a cup of burning meths, warming their frost-

bitten fingers which stuck bloatedly out from their woollen mitts.

We also had a little bottle of meths that we had kept to light a signal fire, and I now had to dig for it in the bottom of the bag. I poured it carefully into the Primus tank, then pulled out the pyjama cord which held up my windproof pants. My cold fingers took ages to feed it through the filler hole. I struck a match. It burst into an initial flare, but did not remain alight.

"Bloody Canadian matches," I cursed. "Why can't anyone make decent ones but us British? Every bit of stick is burn worthy."

"It's a Canadian dodge to prevent a forest fire," answered Roger, laconically, striking another match, with more success. He lit the end of my makeshift wick. A little flame burst into our cold, cheerless environment. Hugh had a better idea. Once we were all in the sleeping-bag, he placed the little stove between us, using our heads as tent poles to keep the fabric off the flame. It presented an extraordinary scene. The yellow light illuminated the boys' faces. Roger's teeth gleamed in the distance at his end of the bag and his eyes shone. Hugh looked wild and hectic like an infuriated Highlander. Both had smiles of pleasure on their faces as if this was the uttermost delight in the world. We talked the hours away until there was no meths left.

Our main topic of conversation was, would we have reached the Pole if the radio had not let us down? Roger reminded us of our slow progress.

"Not as bad as Nares," said Hugh defensively. "There were frequent entries in his men's journal of 'course and distance made good—1½ miles. Distance marched—13 miles'." His fifteen men were dragging 405 pounds apiece on three sledges, and their exertion in the severe cold began to tell. All the party suffered from scurvy, and two of them so badly that they were passengers on the sledge. Instead of advancing with a steady walk, more than half of each day was expended by the men in facing the sledge and dragging it forward a few feet at a time. They reached 83°10′N.—exactly 399½ nautical miles from the Pole.

I ran my tongue over my lips. I had developed a running

sore. Was it scurvy? M'Clintock had grown mustard and cress
during the winters on the *Fox*, to ward off the disease. "Try
chewing my sock," suggested Roger. "Plenty of green mould
there."

One becomes incredibly thirsty when travelling on the polar
pack and usually we satisfied this craving for drink with big
mugs of tea. There was none of that for us now and I awoke in
the night longing for something to quench my raging thirst. I
put up my hand and chipped ice off the walls of the tent. It
tasted of paraffin and the tail-end of six weeks' living, but it was
wet and I sucked it like a lollipop. No wonder I can't sleep, I
thought. It's only 6 p.m. and already we had been in bed for
several hours. Hugh was snoring on one side, and Roger's legs
on the other forced me to lie like a knitting needle. For the first
day since we started our journey I was not physically tired
from the effort of travel and our battles against the elements. I
looked out of the tent. There was a glorious irridescent red
evening sky. It was out of all proportion, a vast limitless space.
I gazed into it, like a gypsy into her crystal ball, willing the wings
of a plane to come into my vision and reflect the sun's rays, a
nice new radio aboard to be left at Ward Hunt. I woke Hugh
up at 11 p.m. and suggested that he go and test the ice. He
vetoed my plan gruffly, spread over my section of the bag, and
started to snore again. But, at 4 a.m., he put forward the same
suggestion.

The sledge was lashed in record time and we pulled it easily
down to the edge of the lead. I longed to hurry on in front to
break the suspense. Had the lead frozen during the hours of the
night? Could it have opened with the movements of the tide?

The situation had changed. Brash ice had piled up on the far
side and there were signs of ice overriding along a diagonal line
across the lead. There was a two-foot wide track of open water
with a slightly stretched-elastic look on the surface. It mean-
dered from our side to that of the land. I looked closely at the
ice on the edge of the lead. It consisted of fern-like crystals jigsawed together with the "flowers" of sea-salt squeezed up to the
surface. The blackness was caused by the proximity of the water
underneath. This kind of ice is called "nilas", a Russian word,
as most polar met. terms are. This is due to the fact that the

Russians were the earliest in this scientific field. Hugh hurled some blocks of ice on to the surface. It shuddered and bent but did not break. "Test it on our skis," I said. "For goodness sake let's go."

"It's only half an inch thick, you know," said Hugh. I thrust in my ski stick and realised with horror that I could push it in right to the hilt. But, undaunted, we all busied ourselves fixing on our planks. Because it was now getting on in April my fingers did not flinch from contact with the metal as I clipped the bindings across my boots. Hugh put an extra length of rope through his harness and slid his feet resolutely forward. This time it was me who urged him to take care, and to keep left, farther away from that gash of open water. The ice bowed slightly beneath his skis. I fixed my eyes on the far side and followed him, with the sledge trundling along behind, making so much noise that one could not hear any cracking of the ice.

Before us was a great expanse of open water with whiffs of smoke puffing up from here and there. Suddenly I got the fright of my life. A head popped up from the middle of a stream of open water right at Hugh's feet. Round, amazed pop-eyes fixed mine. A bearded seal! He looked at us, dived and resurfaced even nearer. He had obviously never seen anything so curious in his life. His whiskers glistened with water and crystal drops rolled off his streamlined brown shoulders. I felt rather as I have done with the proximity of a ship in the middle of a field in Holland—completely out of place on its canal. The seal was mesmerised by our presence and sat there looking at us as though his eyes were about to fall out of his head. I was delighted to see him, though. I felt we were nearly home. We had found something else alive in the world.

A yet darker zone of ice swept round us and lay across our path. I could feel the surface of the ice give as I pushed against my ski sticks, so I shuffled one ski along after the other and put no pressure on my arms. Bolder now, we turned right, parallel to the shore, in order to find an easy access. All that lay between us and the shelf ice was a hundred yards or so of brash and tumbled ice. The shore-line was now developing into a cliff of ice, seventy feet high. As we came level with it, I shivered. It was dark and cold. A shaft of sunlight played on the lead ahead

—a line of weakness in the cliff. We drew parallel with it then Hugh turned at right-angles and gingerly thrust his stick over the final few feet of the ice. With the rise and fall of the tide there was a weak line between the junction of the lead and the cliff.

Water was seeping up here and lying in a pool. I stood, watching Hugh as he untied his bindings and stepped out of his skis. He threw them up over his head on to the shelf ice then hauled himself over the edge. I found myself crying as I followed him and handed him up my skis. I heaved myself up the bank and stood in the sparkling sun. I turned my back on the pack ice, my face towards the hills. Emotions followed each other in a turmoil; frustration, bitter disappointment, relief and thankfulness; deep longing for my children and a fury that I had been prevented from achieving my goal. I had wanted to stand at the North Pole as a justification of the physical effort and all we had put into one journey, but for many other reasons besides. It was bitter publicly to announce one's goal and fall far short. We had had to turn back said Hugh, with conviction. I had never been so sure, and myself would most certainly have pushed on and have been out of food and paraffin by the end of the month, and be dead by now.

It was no time to be emotional. The sledge was still the wrong side of the tide crack. Roger pushed at the back while Hugh hauled at the cow-catcher, and I heaved on the ropes. He lifted it bodily in the air and perched the front of the runners on a block of ice half way up. "Hold it," shouted Roger, "while I climb up." At the same time Hugh's feet slithered on the soft snow. I had a good stance on the shelf ice at the top, but I had not the strength to hold the weight of the sledge by my arms alone. The rope slithered relentlessly through my hands and the sledge thundered back down on to the ice. It all had to be done again. This time I took a belay round the axe, well driven into the snow. Roger's head drew level with Hugh's and then both of them with mine. We were up.

CHAPTER SEVEN

It was a glorious day with the mist hovering over the hills like a hot July morning in the mountains at home. I expected the sun to blaze away the vapour, but the temperature was minus 12 degrees, and I remembered that there would not be much heat in the sun for many months, by other peoples' standards. Walker Hill did not give up its secrets easily. For three hours we skied across the undulating shelf-ice towards its bulk. No sign of a hut. Supposing there aren't any, I thought. Then suddenly the tip of an antenna pierced the horizon and a few minutes later we came over the rim and looked down into a hollow at the foot of the hill. The summer melt pond glinted greenly out at us, and perched above were four huts. I had an urge to kick my skis off, and my trace, and run and explore. Hugh and Roger wanted to plod on with the sledge. "Oh, to hell with you," I cursed them, unclipped myself and ran on, through the oil drums from air drops that littered the scene, as well as various remains of met. screens and radio masts from past scientific projects.

I remembered Cherry-Garrard's description of arriving back at their base after that ghastly journey from Cape Crozier with the three eggs. They hoped someone would see them, would come and help them round the promontory, give them a hand over the tide crack, pull the sledge up the steep final slope. But no one came. No dogs barked. The three explorers did it all themselves. They halted outside and tried to free each other from the frozen harness. The door opened. "Good God! Here is the Crozier party!" exclaimed a voice in horror, and disappeared!

I knew no one would be inside these huts, but had anyone been, to leave a radio? I fumbled with the wire twisted round the door-knob of the first hut but soon had it undone, and I pushed in. Another door led into a room—a cooker, stove, tins of food, a table, a chair and on it a little tin labelled, hospitably, "matches". By this time the others had arrived with the sledge and parked it at the door. "The same stove that we had in Thule," said Roger heading for one in a corner. I turned my attention on the main kitchen-range and looked for somewhere to light it. Hugh moved over to the two clean-looking pressure stoves set neatly on a shelf. After a few minutes of striking matches, we all tumbled to the same conclusion. There was no fuel. "Plenty of drums," I said, running outside. "Come on, quick." Weldy had told me particularly which drums we must not use. Was it red with blue stripes or blue with yellow? We were looking for paraffin. We found everything else besides. Americans insist that they speak English but I have always had my doubts. I was right. The drums we found were labelled "arctic diesel", "aviation gas", "white spirit". Who had ever heard of words like that. It was paraffin that we were after.

"What's lead gas?" I shouted to Roger.

"Heaven knows," he said. "I've got something here called aero-pro."

"I've found JP4, essence and luboil," said Hugh.

In the end we filled all the stoves with "number one fuel oil" and I crossed my fingers, waiting for an explosion. However, with fits and starts, they were all soon giving out heat.

For the first time in forty-seven days I took off my windproofs, then my Hellyhensen top. We had raised the temperature in the hut now to seventy degrees, so I took off my woollen shirt. With the bulk of the clothes removed, my trousers immediately fell down. I realised then how thin I was. There was a mirror in the hut and I looked into it guardedly, expecting to see a careworn, tired old face with signs of exhaustion well ingrained. But I was surprised to see that I looked well, suntanned and freckled as if newly returned from a ski holiday in the Alps. I felt slightly cheated. I did not look like the great explorer after all. I washed my hands, then rather gingerly my face. It felt most peculiar. Hugh looked wild and woolly, with black hair and beard running into each other. Roger, his beard scanty, looked like a benign smuggler in a school production of *The Pirates of Penzance*.

Now I turned my attention to find some food. Plaisted's

American expedition had been here last, as was evident from
the shelves. I mixed three packets of "vanilla malt" into a
mug and drank the lot at one go. I ate two tins of oysters; then I
found some asparagus tips, a packet of orange-juice powder,
and a "tootie-fruity" bar. Hugh was eating a jelly mix and
Roger, "pie-filling" which he said meant turnip mixed with
semolina. Suddenly we had enough of the American nursery
pap food that U.S. adult citizens go in for. We cleared pancake
mixes and sickly syrups and instant breakfasts right out of the
way and, far at the back, found an old bag of flour, then some
yeast and got down to making bread.

Humphries, an Australian adventurer, had flown in here too.
Instead of the American skimmed milk with all the goodness
taken out, to prevent the American arteries from decaying, we
found an Australian tin labelled "enriched" and genuine
freeze-dried meat.

We weighed the sleeping-bag before hanging it out to dry
and found that two gallons of water had to come out before it
would return to its normal weight. The tent too was nearly
twice its normal weight with ice. It now weighed 46 pounds as
opposed to the 25 pounds at the start. I turned my attention to
clearing up the hut. With the heat of our stove, water was
pouring down from the roof, and drifted snow which had collected on all the shelves was now flowing over the floor. In
order to get some space we started moving the American
expedition's belongings to one side. The shelves were full of
medicines, powders, ointments and injections; everything from
high-powered antibiotics to intestinal speeders up and slowers
down, pain killers and sleeping pills, vitamin tablets by the
dozen.

"Why don't the Americans leave the natural products in the
food and do without the pills?" I asked Hugh. I even found a
cure for gout.

The huts belonged to the Ellesmere Island Ice-shelf Expedition of 1960, a joint project of the American and Canadian
Governments. The expedition had been mainly concerned with
mapping and glaciology in the Ward Hunt area, and reflected
the interest that has been re-aroused in the ice-shelf, now that
oil has been found off the Alaskan coast.

I went outside to get more snow to melt for washing. A blast of sunshine forced me to close my eyes—dazzling snow. Already, after only hours in the hut, I had forgotten how glorious the Arctic could be. Crystal-clear blue skies, white virginal snow. Around the corner of the hut came trotting a delightful little fox. It was pure white, hunched up in a thick white fur coat with spindly little legs sticking out at the bottom. Not the least bit afraid, it looked at me and came closer. I had wanted a fox skin from the co-op at Resolute but now that I saw this little creature walking about, I knew that I could never wear one round my neck. It looked at me again, then pattered off in the sunlight, its feet twinkling on the snow which lay round the hut. Empty tins littered round the door, a skirt of smuts already lay on the snow from the rusty chimney and I felt guilty as I looked up at the cloud of black smoke that was polluting the crystal-clear pure air. How dare we mess up this glorious, uncluttered, empty North, I thought.

Life was already getting complicated. We had to wash up. I felt obliged to take off a few layers of clothes for bed. I had washed my face once today already, but felt that I must do it again. After only eight hours, I rather longed for the simplicity of our camping life. The heat in the hut was eating into me. Relaxation and sleepiness were slowly creeping over me from my feet up. It was marvellous not to have to fight the elements. That night I had the sleeping bag to myself. It was glorious to be able to stretch my legs and turn round, bend my knees if I wanted to or put my head inside. But we had to face the fact that we still had a long, long way to go. There was no generator waiting for us in the Ward Hunt hut, nor was there any other means of making our own radio work. Our nearest neighbours were 120 miles away at Alert.

"Don't forget we have been officially forbidden to go anywhere near there," reiterated Hugh.

"But surely," I said, "they could not refuse to carry a message?"

Hugh was against it. "They must be getting worried back at Resolute," he said. "And Weldy will be asked to come and see if we are here. Let's give them a day. We are due a bit of self indulgence."

Restlessly, I reluctantly agreed.

I strolled out of the hut that evening and began to climb
Mount Walker. The sun was a deep red disc. Lumps of rock
were showing through the snow. I picked up a pebble and it
was marvellous to hold it in my hand after weeks of snow and
ice. A fossil was etched on one side. In some age these hills had
been green. Lichen had now tinged the rocks scarlet and crystals
of green tourmaline caught my eye. As the gradient increased, I
felt more at home and became alive. Mountains are really my
mecca, not the horizontal pack. Hills unfolded to the east. They
were beautifully sculptured in shades of soft white. The geo-
graphy of the island of Ward Hunt became clear, the shelf ice
surrounding it like a skirt of rippling snow, with the pack ice
behind as far back as Disraeli Fjord. One of the most seldom-
looked-at views in the world, I thought. No one had lived here
since the early migration of Eskimos. Scientists occasionally
visit it in May and June, but nobody else. On the summit of
Mount Walker I turned about to face the frozen sea. To travel
on it looked impossible, yet we had been there a hundred miles
out. Already it seemed rather a dream. At my back was the land
and over there beyond these mountains lay Alert.

That evening I talked Hugh into falling in with my plan.
Hugh and I would ski to Alert alone. Roger still had painful
frostbitten feet, and someone should stay in case the plane flew
over the hut. We must travel fast. That meant carrying a
minimum load. We would take no tent or sledge, in fact nothing
but a sleeping-bag and a little food. I filled a bag with raisins
and dried milk while Hugh poured fuel into the Primus tank. I
hoped it was not aviation gas. Then he tied the luggage on to
our aluminium pack-frames and we were ready to go.

"Cheerio, Rog," I said as we set off. He looked like the
Ancient Mariner as we left him standing outside the hut, his
hair awry and his feet bare. We expected to take five days. I
pushed on my sticks and my skis slid over the snow. The sun
blazed down on us and the scenery was magnificent. Our
intention was to skim across the top of the map of Canada, to
edge along the northern tip of Ellesmere. We travelled fast, our
light cross-country skis purring along as we lifted our heels for
the next step. This must be the best Nordic ski route in the

world, I thought as I tore along behind Hugh. The hours went by fast.

"Twenty miles up when we round that cape," said Hugh, consulting his map. Cape Aldrich loomed ahead, a glacier thrown over its shoulder like whipped cream, and a magnificent cliff rearing its head beyond.

"Once we are past that, let's lie down for the night," I shouted at Hugh, and he agreed.

At ten o'clock we drew to a halt. With no tent it is difficult to decide where to unravel one's sleeping bag. I felt I needed some territorial rights so I stuck my skis and sticks in a square in the snow. Hugh gingerly lit the Primus while I stamped down the snow and then unrolled the bag. Once in, we lay on our sides with the Primus between and relished our raisins. It was glorious lying there with nothing between my face and the sky. The Arctic was silent and I felt what a privilege it was for us to be there.

After four hours we were cold and set off once more. All the frustrations of the polar journey now fell away as we covered the distance towards Alert. It was marvellous to be able to move, to push on at the speed that one wanted to travel. The surface was excellent, just gently rippling, nothing to hold us back. A bay opened up on our right, Markham Inlet which Peary had visited in 1906. Mountains tumbled towards it to the south and a great glacier swept down at the rear. I longed for time to explore. Cape Nares now lay ahead, its steep cliffs rearing straight up out of the sea.

"I hope there is a ledge for us to ski round," I said looking up.

Nares' party had come this way in May of 1876. Not the leader himself, but Lieut. Aldrich. They had left their ship, the *Alert*, in Lady Franklin Bay on the east coast of Ellesmere, looking towards Greenland. One sledge party was to force a way into the ice and attain the highest northern latitude possible, and to ascertain the possibility of a more fully equipped expedition reaching the North Pole via that route. This party was under Commander Markham. The second sledge party, under Aldrich, was to explore the north coast. He had fourteen men to help, and one other lieutenant, and each man dragged 242 pounds. They set off on a calm day, with the temperature

at minus 45 degrees Fahrenheit. They shot four hares on the
first day, and ate them at once, little realising that this was all
the fresh meat they were to see. Soft snow gave them "severe
labour in advancing the sledges", as Aldrich wrote in his
report. He was bitterly disappointed to find the land falling
back south after they rounded Cape Columbia, as he had
hoped that his party might have outdone Markham's in
northerlying! However, they slogged on along the coast, in
misty dank weather. It was often difficult to decide if they were
travelling on land or sea, and the sledge constantly came to a
full stop in deep soft snow.

Aldrich wrote in his diary at this point: "The men are all very
much done up, the fact being that, light loads or heavy loads,
this thick snow takes it out of one tremendously and the constant standing pulls shake one to pieces." They had to relay,
which is soul-destroying work, as we knew only too well!
Aldrich remarked that he often had not the heart to tell the
men that, after nine hours work, they had actually only covered
two and a half miles from that morning's camp! But on they
went, Aldrich striding ahead of the men, and shouting, "Main
topsail, haul," to urge them on when the sledge ground to a
halt. By now the men were all complaining of swollen legs and
Aldrich realised that scurvy was getting the better of them.
Drifting snow, which stung their faces, slowed them down
even more, but Aldrich was enchanted to pick up a leaf of
willow, showing that somewhere something was green and
growing. The men talked of England, fresh meat and vegetables.

Aldrich turned back at a point he called Yelverton Bay,
82°16′N, 85°33′W. The party celebrated with grog and biscuits,
and unfurled the Union Jack. The journey back was dreadful—
at one point it took an hour to advance ten yards! Heavy snow,
dense fog and the scurvy-ridden invalids all kept the party
back, but eventually they staggered into a search party and
were helped back to the *Alert*, climbing aboard at midnight
amid cheers and congratulations. One of the crew made up a
poem in true Victorian style:

"Welcome home to the wished for rest
 Traveller to North and traveller to West
 Welcome back from bristling floes
 Frowning cliff and quaking snow
 Nobly, bravely the work was done
 Inch by inch was the hard fight won
 . . . .
 Rough and rude is the feast we bring
 Rougher and ruder the verse we sing
 Not rough, not rude are the thoughts that rise
 To choke our voices and dim our eyes,
 As we call to mind that joyous sight
 On an April morning cold and bright
 When the chosen band stepped boldly forth
 To an unknown West and an unknown North.
 . . . ."

The entire expedition now scoured the area for fresh meat to cure the invalids, and their health rapidly improved.

I was thinking that at least we had not had scurvy to contend with, when I suddenly realised that there was a moving object in the sky. Heading for us!

"Look, there's a bird!" I shouted to Hugh, when I at last found my voice. He whipped round, to follow my quivering arm.

"No, no, it's a plane," he shouted. "Quick, quick, get your rocket." Already he was yanking his out of his pocket.

I fumbled in my front kangaroo pouch for the rocket that I had carried ever since we had left Resolute. I had intended to fire it off in the face of any attacking polar bear. Now my fingers closed on the icy-cold metal, the paper cover had disintegrated long ago. At last I forced it out of my pocket, and pulled on the thin cord at the top. I was mesmerised by the plane, my eyes riveted to it, my whole comprehension involved in that moving thing in the sky. It had been our sky up to that instant . . . nothing had come into our vision for all these weeks when we had been alone. But the plane passed by and left me destitute.

Over the snow, at my feet was a scattering of purple powder. My flare had been a damp squib. The plane soared away round the coast and vanished into the sun.

"Oh hell," I thought. "I do not want to be rescued anyway. I would much rather finish our journey round to Alert."

But Hugh had more faith in the plane than me. He poured the aero-fuel out of the Primus into the bag that contained our meagre food. I wanted to push on and keep warm but Hugh insisted on lighting a bonfire. And he soon had a stream of black smoke pouring up into the crystal-clear air. Meanwhile I was freezing and getting cross. But Hugh was right. Looking back towards the sun a tiny little fly came out of the sky. It was the plane again. It circled us twice, getting lower and lower. Then I thought it was going to sweep down Markham Inlet and forget all about us. But I was wrong. There was a great roaring and shuddering as it put down on the snow by our side.

As the blizzard of snow it had created settled, I saw a figure coming towards us. It was Roger walking carefully on his sore feet, John Mossman was at his side. Behind him was the stocky figure of Weldy, and he said matter-of-factly, "You were making good time."

Without delay, and silently, we bundled into the plane. Roger handed up the skis and our little luggage for five days. Weldy revved his engines and lifted his plane off the glacier back into the sky. I sat absolutely silent. We are going due south I said to myself, not north. I pressed my face against the window and gazed down at the glorious mountains of northern Canada, my mind numbed. After several hours' flight we saw the lights of Resolute village twinkling in the sun. Weldy skimmed his plane low over the little houses and put down on the runway at the base. It was 1 a.m. I looked out. Three little children stood in a group beside the huts. Sandra held a little bundle in her arms—Rory. I couldn't bear to get out of the plane and face them. I pushed Hugh out first. I forget now what I was really waiting for. Then I made myself follow him. As soon as I got down the steps, six arms were thrown round my neck.

"Did you not get to the North Pole then?" were the first

words Robin said. "Oh Mummy, does that mean you are going off again."

"No, no," I said, clutching all of them at once. But the words stuck in my throat because somehow I knew that I would find a way to give myself another chance.

"Don't cry, Mum," said Bruce. "I'll get the Pole for you, if you want it so badly."

CHAPTER EIGHT

We HAD LOST our geographical aim, the North Pole, and with it, our financial support. The *Daily Telegraph* was no longer interested in us or our ambitions. However, Hugh's medical research undertaking jigsawed into an international project. He could not morally withdraw his participation and abandon it now.

We surveyed our situation back in Sudlavenik's little hut, around the stove.

We had food for three more months. We had camping equipment. Hugh had all that was necessary for his research project. Provided the *Daily Telegraph* were prepared to pay our way home, we could complete Hugh's project on our own resources.

To our astonishment the *Telegraph* cabled "No". The morale of our party was low. We had failed to reach the Pole, but we had succeeded in returning safely to land. No credit was forthcoming for this, in spite of the fact that we could have cost our sponsors thousands of pounds in search and rescue. This was fair enough, but their attitude now was to me the last straw.

Seething with outrage I sent my reply, "Surely even a defeated football team is allowed home in the chartered bus." This brought the rejoinder that Roger and Sandra could be funded home, but not Hugh and me!

"Oh, well," said Hugh, quite unmoved. "The American Space Research Authorities or NASA, as they call themselves, think highly of my project, and are very involved with the results. I'll get on to them. All I need for my work is an uninhabited island north of the Arctic Circle so that the sun remains high in the sky. And some volunteer guinea pigs, you, you and you."

It is difficult to raise money when two thousand miles north of the source. We hung around Resolute, dejected and weary, waiting for a reply from Minnesota University. Roger and I were particularly glum. We avoided the "told you so" faces of the Europeans at the Base, and could not tolerate the idle, cheerful chatter of the Eskimos in the village.

There is nothing so dead as a failed expedition, I thought, as I dolefully made scones for the children's tea, trying to fill in an afternoon. I heard footsteps squeaking on the snow outside. Hugh pushed open the inner door before closing the outer, letting in a blast of cold air. I turned round to curse him, and saw his beaming face.

"The Americans have turned up trumps. £1,500 provided I expand the programme to include some extra data on rhythms of particular interest to them. Mental acuity and muscle strength at different times of the day."

The morale of the party began to rise as if a pound of yeast had been added to its blood. Hugh's news had the same effect on me as when the sun rose over the horizon and returned to us on the polar pack, that far off day in February.

We laid a map of the Canadian Arctic Islands on the floor and all sat down on hands and knees, weighing up the possibilities.

Weldy's plane would have to be chartered to take us to our island. He charged getting on for £2 a mile, so our radius was limited to our budget.

"I've always wanted to go back to Devon Island in the Spring," said Roger. "Wally Herbert and I put in there after our dog sledge journey from Greenland. Musk ox, walrus. Glorious place."

"Right," said Hugh. "That's fixed then."

Sandra opted out: Ken, in true Mountie tradition, had captured his girl. It was a blow to Hugh's research, but she had kept the children happy in our absence, and we were unreservedly grateful for that.

Another day, and we were off. It was the first of May. We jolted down the snow on the runway, then Weldy's Otter lifted itself into the air and Cornwallis Island fell away below. Soon the base was only a black smudge on the sparkling snow. I clutched Rory on my knee and tried to justify it all to myself, and to review our reasons for setting out into the blue again.

Why risk oneself, family and future? Society looks for security, but there is a perverse human quality of inventing new insecurities as fast as the old ones are eliminated. In fact, insecurity is deep in the roots of vitality itself and when it no longer challenges, no response will follow and knowledge will come to a full stop. However, even explorers are self-preservationists at heart and the satisfaction of a journey lies in avoiding dangers, not at deliberately putting oneself at risk. An explorer always expects to come home.

A research project represents the intellectual side of an expedition. It can assume an obsessional fetish, as with Cherry-Garrard and Wilson, who carried their emperor penguin's eggs all the way back through "the worst journey in the world". Garrard himself wrote, "we travelled for science! These three small embryos from Cape Crozier, that weight of fossils from Buckly Island, that mass of material, less spectacular but gathered just as carefully, hour by hour, in wind and drift, darkness and cold, was striven for in order that the world may have a little more knowledge, that it may build on what it knows instead of on what it thinks."

After all the effort that Garrard's party put into the finding of the eggs, when Cherry-Garrard visited the Natural History Museum a few years later with Scott's sister, and asked to see the eggs, the custodian flatly denied that any such eggs were in existence, let alone in their possession!

Cherry-Garrard also remarked "that some of our men, particularly the scientists, were ambitious; some wanted money; some a help up the scientific ladder; others a name; others an F.R.S. Why not? But we had men who did not care a rap for money or fame."

This was even more true of Scott's party, who hung on to their thirty pounds of fossils gathered on the Beardmore glacier after the party were down to three—Bowers, Wilson and Scott himself—and they had no strength left to slog on any more. If the sledge had only carried food and tent, couldn't they have made those extra eleven miles to their depot in spite of the storm? We ourselves had carried Hugh's urine samples all those sick ening miles back to land after our radio broke down. Nowadays, even more than in Scott's time, the word "science" is considered magic and justifies anything, expense, time and danger.

However, I was going to Devon Island because I wanted to

see the spring spreading over an Arctic Island, jostling it into life and pouring vitality into its heart, to feel the sun in the high summer, to watch it melt the snow and expose enough land for a bird to nest and a lemming to find a morsel to eat.

The excited chatter of the children made more moralising impossible. "Are we there yet?" asked Rona, two minutes after departure.

"Look, look," shouted the boys peering out of the window. "I can see a bear."

"Rubbish," I said, "It's the Base Bombadier."

Scott used to say that the worst part of an expedition was over when the preparations were finished. How right he was. It is great to know that any uncompleted tasks have to go by the board.

Devon Island is icebound, but the island was a part of the hunting and migrating route that led northwards from the barren lands of Canada proper into Baffin Island, over to Devon, then along Eureka Sound through Ellesmere Island to Greenland. So, four hundred years ago, many Eskimo families were dotted along the shore—but nobody lives there now.

We had chosen the north-easterly coast to make our summer camp at Cape Sparbo. Cook had wintered here in a cave after his return from the North Pole. He and his two Eskimos had struggled ashore in late September with their supplies nearly exhausted. They had only five bullets left, although Cook afterwards confessed that he had one more hidden in his pocket. The land was bleak, but they survived the winter quite happily and then set off in the spring to cross to Greenland, where Cook had his first bath in fourteen months. He was still faced with a dangerous 600-mile journey south before reaching a Danish settlement at Upernarvik, so he decided to leave all his navigation instruments and records to come later by boat. So went Cook's story. From Upernarvik he travelled by ship to a larger settlement, and then by steamer to Copenhagen. The ship, the *Hans Egede*, put into Scotland at Lerwick, and it was from here that Cook sent the message announcing his discovery and claiming the Pole. When the *Hans Egede* sailed into Copenhagen, newspaper reporters besieged Cook in the dining saloon. Among them was Peter Freuchen, acting temporary reporter for

Politiken. "I don't know how it happened," he said later, "but after the first few minutes I was convinced that something was seriously wrong with his story." Freuchen's paper, having arranged a banquet in honour of Cook, rejected his article, pointing out that they could hardly dine him and call him a fraud at the same time. During this dinner a slip of paper was shoved under Cook's plate. It was a copy of a message. "Stars and stripes nailed to the North Pole—Peary."

The Arctic Institute of North America has a hut near Cape Sparbo, with a runway. It was to be visited by scientists in July and August. As Hugh would find their plane useful to take out his specimens, we decided to make use of the scientists and to stay in that area, just to the west of Cape Sparbo, instead of at Cook's camping spot itself.

"There's the hut," yelled back the pilot, and sure enough I could make out a black blob more uniform than the other black blobs that represented rocks. We put down gently in a flurry of snow. The children exploded out of the plane. I followed and jumped down into knee-deep dry powder snow. There was a stillness in the air: the island was waiting for spring.

"It's our island. Our own, our own," shouted the children as we unloaded the plane. Their faces haloed in white fox fur, the cold crisp air had put vitality into russet cheeks already.

"Look at Rory, he's crawled out of his bag," said Rona. I had overlooked the difficulties. Rory was no longer a sweet little cuddly baby lying in his cot. He was now a mobile terror. But we had lived through this stage three times before and, in spite of a toddler, I had never missed a weekend on the hills at home.

"Help get a tent pitched so that there is somewhere to put him," I shouted to the boys. They buckled to, enjoying being needed.

Empty, now, Weldy's plane revved up and was gone. It circled us once, dipped its wings, then disappeared into the grey line that joined the land and sea at the horizon.

"You got everything, Mum?" asked Rona.

"Hell, I meant to get another five pounds of flour from the co-op," I remembered.

"You couldn't have, it's gone bust again," answered Robin.
As one of the community at Resolute he knew everything.
"William McKenzie trained a new white manager, but his
Indian wife refused to live with the Eskimos so he's gone off
and left it in a mess. Did I tell you too, Pudluk's got a new
baby but they've given it to Noah's sister who had a baby but
it wasn't her husband's so it's gone to its own Dad's wife who is
Pudluk's wife's sister. Get it?'

"No," said Roger. "I'm all confused."

The Arctic Institute hut was of the Nissen type. We left a store
of food alongside it, then we loaded up the sledge. I clipped the
children's ski bindings over their sealskin kamiks and we set off
towards the shore. Land ran into sea. I couldn't make out the
margin. I skied along behind the sledge, Rory, on my back,
chortling with delight. I felt a surge of enthusiasm. We were at
home in this environment. The children were harnessed like
husky dogs and the sledge trundled along behind. Robin's
trace was taut, but Bruce, I noticed, was inclined to take a
snide ride in the sledge. Rona's little legs pumped her skis
along bravely, trying to keep up. Their Eskimo anoraks of
dark cherry were just the right tone for the scene. We skied over
the gentle undulations of soft banks of snow that had rounded
all contours in the valley, which was held by a half-moon
escarpment of rock—2,000 feet high. Above this the ice cap,
glittering and greenly white in the sun, holding Devon Island
down in an ice age similar to Scotland's thousands of years
ago.

After a mile we came across an exposed narrow crescent
of rough dolerite. It was great to rest one's eyes from the
reflection of the snow.

"Here's the place," I shouted with conviction, over the noise
of six pairs of skis squeaking over the snow. The others agreed.
Our base tent was a three-man pyramid type, two layers of
cotton trapping a wall of warm air between. This was our home.
The boys had the north pole tent, and Roger the experimental
one of double nylon. Rona and Rory were to sleep with Hugh
and me. As I unrolled the sleeping-bag I thought of the Persian
proverb "where lies my carpet there is my home". We all set
about organising our goods and chattels. The less one owns, the

Rona Simpson (7) and her Eskimo classmates, Resolute Bay School.
April, 1969.

Robin, Bruce and Rona Simpson plus Eskimo friend Noah. On the
sea-ice near Resolute Bay village, Cornwallis Island, N.W.T.
April, 1969.

Roger Tufft, Robin Simpson (9) and Bruce Simpson (8) out skiing on Jones Sound sea-ice off Cape Sparbo, June, 1969.

more important one's few belongings become. Like prison camp inmates, each stowed away pencil stubs and slips of paper written only on one side. I had once watched nuns on a train packing and repacking their small bags of worldly possessions, turning the few articles over as if they were gold in their hands.

The fourth tent was devoted to Hugh's research. Rhythms of potassium and sodium are geared to the twenty-four hour clock. What happens if one tries a routine squashed into a twenty-one hour day?

Many of man's internal functions run rhythmically each day. It used to be thought that this was just an obvious consequence of the earth's twenty-four hour period of rotation. The fact that it was obviously convenient to be up and active during the day and asleep during the dark seemed common sense. However, over the past few years, experiments—especially on human beings living for long periods down caves—have shown that these rhythms are mainly due to an internal mechanism like the heart-beat, though this is prompted by the environment, so that the rhythm gives the right phase at the right time. Now, in our experiment, we were to fit eight days and nights into a normal week to see what would happen to the intrinsic rhythm—whether this amount of adjustment was possible or whether the rhythm would just give up, and run at its own speed, which is usually a little more than twenty-four hours. This is not just an academic question. It happens every time a plane is eastbound, flying through $45°$ of longitude per day— for instance, flying from London to Leningrad. We know—and the pilot knows—that this makes one feel "out of sorts", but the question is to assess objectively just "how much". Accordingly, on Devon, while on this speeded schedule, we were to make regular tests of mental acuity by measuring the time taken to sum random numbers, by dexterity tests of threading fifteen pairs of beads into a small hole, and by estimating as accurately as possible one minute against a stop-watch. This is concerned with the appreciation of the passage of time. Normally subjects overestimate in the morning and underestimate in the afternoon. Obviously, time perception is important to pilots in gauging the rate at which things are happening. Pulse and blood pressure and muscle tone were further variables

E

that the U.S. Air Force were particularly interested in and we were to measure these every three hours.

In addition, Hugh was measuring the rates at which the body excretes sodium, potassium and chloride, and adrenal hormones under the circumstances of the twenty-one hour day; this was to amplify and extend results of his 1960 Spitzbergen experiment, which had shown little acceptance of the twenty-one hour rhythm in the eight subjects studied—a poor outlook for us mortals with any ambition of living on other celestial bodies than our own, if they are revolving at a different speed. An important new point about our Devon experiment was that the children were to participate. Could it be that they are more adaptable than adults in respect of rhythms, or not? In other words, has the body inherited the twenty-four hour rhythm or has it "learnt" about it by living on earth. Current evidence suggests inheritance as an important factor in the "circadian" rhythms, but Hugh was looking for some proof.

During the early weeks of May, we had a struggle to maintain enough heat in the tent, to keep track of the children's gloves and socks, and to teach Rona arithmetic. Roger took over the boys a few hours at a time. He taught them his own subjects enthusiastically—English Literature and English Modern History—and for the first time I was jolted into the realisation that my children knew more than I did.

I enjoyed the domestic chores and pottering about, after the struggle on the polar pack. It had left me weary, tired in my bones and mentally exhausted too. My wants were limited to the environment. The greatest luxury I craved for was running water. I had had enough of chipping ice and scooping billy-cans of snow.

On the last day of May I heard a noise. It took me a moment to realise the significance. It had not been made by one of us! In the dead world of Devon Island, only we or the wind broke the silence. There was nothing else. But now I heard the unmistakable sound of twittering.

"Mum, come quickly!" shouted Rona, breathless, thrusting her head through the tent door. I left the bucket full of frozen nappies thawing on the Primus and looked out. Rory was perched on the children's little sledge, and was laughing and pointing at a black and white bird, fluttering over the snow, cheerfully twittering a repetitive jingle. "A snow bunting," stated Robin. "I've seen it before in Glencoe."

I felt a strange elation. The spring; when everything happens that is worth happening. The children were susceptible too. They were scampering off, shouting. They rolled in the snow, pushing each other over, laughing, tossing handfuls of snow at each other's face. They kicked their feet in the air, somersaulted and tumbled as if the spring breeze was whispering in their blood. It whipped invitingly about their hair. The three of them lifted their heads to it, threw out their arms and ran off, skipping and falling about and laughing hilariously.

I picked up Rory and automatically pulled off his layers of breeks till I reached his soggy nappy. Clouds of steam rose as it met the cold air. I tossed it aside as usual, but instead of instantly freezing, it remained limp. The thaw had come! Sure enough, water was collecting around the tent. I could fill the billy-can! Life was easing up.

The snow now retreated fast, and a narrow strip of land appeared along the crest of each undulation of the raised beach, and the island began to breathe again.

Our valley was a series of these raised beaches, each representing a fall in the level of the tide every four hundred or so years. The currently accepted theory is that the ice cap is melting, so less weight is holding the island down into the sea. As it rises up out of the water, a new beach is formed. The children found fossils to bear this out, coiled worms and shells, several miles up from the coast. We forgot about lesson time with the excitement of wandering about on dry land.

Hugh abandoned his research for a day and he and Roger set off to explore the easterly limits of our glen. They were soon out of sight and I retreated to the tent to change the baby.

"Look, big dogs over there," I heard Rona say.

"Wolves, wolves," Robin shouted, an instant later. "Nine of them."

My heart froze. I pushed Rory to the back of the tent and forced myself to look out. I blinked as the brilliant sunshine blinded me after the gloom of the tent.

Sure enough, nine huge shaggy well-fed looking creatures

were walking in Indian file across the snow in our direction. Anywhere else they would be Alsatians, but here they must be wolves.

"Shall I get the camera?" asked Bruce, in a normal voice.

"No, get the gun," I shouted. "It's in Roger's tent. He said he would leave it fully loaded."

The wolves came nearer, lifting their feet high in the soft snow. Rory, abandoned in the tent, began to howl for attention.

"Shut up, Rory," I ordered over my shoulder in a trembling voice. "The wolves will hear you."

The baby shrieked even louder as Rona slapped his fat leg. The leading wolf stopped in his tracks. He lifted his head and sniffed. He looked me straight in the eye and then turned and led his retinue diagonally away from the tent.

"Here's the gun," said Bruce, "but the bullets have fallen out and I've lost them in the snow."

The last wolf looked longingly in our direction, hesitated, then reluctantly followed suit.

Weak-kneed, I pushed the children into the tent and clutched them to me in my arms.

"Let go, you're squashing," complained Rona, her shrill voice directly in my ear.

"I'll light the Primus and make some tea," said Robin, enjoying acting "Dad".

"I'll go out and keep watch," bravely announced Bruce, who is petrified of ghosts at home. Children grow up early when close to the environment, I thought to myself. I had never known my boys so intimately before. Home work, cubs, music lessons, TV, or a gaggle of friends in to play, insulate the city mother from her children's personalities.

Snug in the tent, I spooned powdered milk into the children's tea. I was happy. Rory cuddled up to me, which meant he was sleepy and unlikely to go on the rampage. The previous day he had upset the six-pound tin of jam into his sleeping bag, and then played with it as if it were plasticine. Rona's golden hair hung about her face. She was writing in our "Devon Island Notes". I looked at the dog-eared book.

I HAV SEN 4 SNOW DUNTINS. THEY AER BLEK AND WIET AND SININ HAPEELEE BEECOS IT IS SPRIN.

Summer camp, Devon Island, N.W.T. Robin and Bruce Simpson between sledge and tent. Old squaw ducks on lake. July, 1969.

Rona's seventh birthday cake at Cape Sparbo camp, Devon Island, N.W.T. With Rory ($1\frac{1}{2}$), Robin and Bruce. Midsummer, 1969.

Robin and Bruce play on ice-floes on Jones Sound, off Devon Island. July, 1969.

Wasn't it more important to know about the spring than how to spell? Or should they be at school in Glasgow? Had I made them drop-outs from life?

Robin was pulling on his gloves. "I've got to do Rog's met. ob. at 0015. Come on Bruce."

"I'll just stay here," said his brother, "and get on with the barometrical pressure graph. I want to find the average of the temps for May before Rog comes back," he added, looking knowledgeable and far more than eight.

Robin's round red face came back through the tent door, a little boy's face, mixed with adult responsibility.

"Make some scones, Mum. I'm starving."

A wet dough of flour, water, baking powder and raisins dolloped into a frying-pan and cooked in seal fat makes a delicious "scone". I set to work. Everything I needed was at arm's reach. Housekeeping is easy under these conditions. I pulled down a nappy, drying at the apex of the tent, to turn out my nicely browned offering. In all my years of experience I have come to the conclusion that germs just do not exist under camping conditions. Nappies dipped in icy streams do not cause the sore bottoms that develop at home after careful laundering. Lack of wash up does not produce food poisoning, and no soap and water does not result in itches and spots. Like every family we have experienced all these irritations at home.

Robin came back. "There are creatures about. Little eyes peeping at me."

I looked out. My eyes swept the horizon. Nothing stirred.

"There," said Robin. "Too late it's gone. There! Oh, you've missed it again."

Intrigued we all trooped out of the tent. Robin led us to the spot.

Minute footprints zigzagged over the snow. They started from a one-inch hole in the surface and finished at another.

"There!" screamed Rona. I wheeled round. Missed it again. We crouched down and watched.

There was a noise like a turbine from under the snow. Then—a pair of whiskers broke the surface, and a little fat mousy face with flat ears and small round black piercing eyes looked out. The head revolved several times making sure that the coast was clear. Then out popped the little grey animal, the size of a mouse, and confidently sauntered over the snow. It's body was chunky and ended in a sprout of a tail.

Rory had seen it! He burst into an excited chatter. The animal went into a frenzy. It stood on its hind legs, hissing and squeaking, hair erect and teeth bared. It hopped up and down in a fury, its body hunched up, head and hindquarters raised, forelegs extended. Rona ran towards it, hands outstretched. It made no attempt to escape, but squared up pugnaciously, snarling, feinting and growling. It jumped fully nine inches into the air, then threatened again, gnashing its teeth. The intensity of its rage astonished me. It made short jerky movements towards Rona. It flew at her boot trying to bite and she withdrew hastily. At that the creature trotted off, paused frequently to look at us, then suddenly kicked out a flurry of snow with its hind feet, belted the snow with its head, the noise of steam turbines started again, and the little animal vanished down a tunnel it made as it went along, head first, without apparent effort.

"It's a hamster," said Bruce.

"No, a lemming," I corrected.

The lemming is an Arctic animal, found right round the world in Scandinavia, the Soviet Union, Alaska, Canada, Greenland, but not Iceland. The two species found on the Canadian Archipelago are called the "brown" and the "varying" lemming. According to Eskimo folklore lemmings fall out of the sky. Their admiration for the creature took the form of making amulets with the skin from the skull. A special kayak variety endowed the owner with the ability to breathe life into it when necessary, so that the spirit of the lemming came to his aid and gave him a superhuman turn of speed with his paddle. Young boys used to have amulets made from the animal's feet as this would ensure they grew up as clever and fast when building snow houses as the lemming in building passages in the snow.

Greenland Eskimos have a more practical use for the lemmings today. They had told me that a lemming pelt placed face down on a frost-bitten sore would peel off the gangrenous skin. In Resolute I had noticed a pile of the soft little skins in Pudluk's house. They were waiting for the birth of the expected baby, and would be used as a bandage for its umbilical cord and as nappies for its early days.

"Let's dig it out and eat it," said Robin, interrupting my line of thought. Sure enough I remembered Freuchen writing of the Eskimos roasting lemmings between two flat stones, but reporting that the meat had a sweet rather sickly taste.

"No," said Rona. "It's got a nice face when it's not cross. Just like you, Mum. But why has it gone down to the dark, out of the sun?"

It was far warmer under the snow, I explained. Two feet down it can be as much as 22 degrees warmer than at the surface. To cope with the cold, lemmings do not hibernate, but grow a winter coat of long hair that covers the woolly under-fur. Air, a non-heat-conductor, is trapped among the dense fur, and the long outer hair prevents the warm air from escaping. Its streamlined, compact body, short tail, rounded head and tiny ears reduce heat loss too. But it has to be active to maintain its body temperature and needs plenty of food in order to expend a considerable part of its metabolic energies in heat production.

About three feet under the snow the lemming will build a nest, in a carefully chosen spot, so well insulated that the temperature inside it may reach 50 degrees Fahrenheit even when it's away below zero outside. From here he will make a series of tunnels leading to food. Lemmings have been known to eat twice their own weight in grass every twenty-four hours. An animal weighing less than two ounces would eat about a hundredweight per year. Norwegian hunters have called them "fat, busy, agile, mowing machines".

My eyes were caught by a patch of green. My heart stirred. There had been no green in my seven months' world of white and blue. I took Rona's hands and we ran towards it. Wet, thawing snow had avalanched below our camp, exposing a bank of rocks and below it a level patch of green. Another lemming was running over the newly exposed grass.

"A ball," said Rona, picking up a globular shaped mass of hay. "Oh, it's got babies! But they are all dead."

It was a lemming's nest. To make it the lemming had gnawed

grass stems about one inch long and worked it like a gypsy basket. It was reinforced with moss and grey fur. Inside it was clean and sweet and free from droppings.

Three tiny scraggy young lemmings lay in a huddle. Their thin fur clung to them, soggy and wet.

"They've drowned," I said. Melting snow must have swept the nest from its safe cranny below the bank. The Arctic is merciless. It sorts out the weaklings and disposes of them in its own harsh way.

Bruce stood waving frantically from a little way off. "More lemmings," he yelled. Quite unmoved by his shrill voice a lemming sat on his haunches, currying the fur on his flanks, shoulders and cheeks with one sweeping forward movement of its front paws. Eyeing him with admiration, crouched a smaller lemming. "It's his girl friend," said Bruce knowingly. "I've been watching."

The larger, male, uttered a series of short squeaks. The female joined in with so much squeaking on her part that the sound was of a continuous trill. The male then ran up to her, pressed one cheek close to her nose, then the other. She pawed his head for a moment, then dashed off, with him in pursuit. They halted a bit away and she allowed him to approach again.

Suddenly, another male lemming appeared on the scene! The first turned with lightning speed, hair erect giving the illusion of twice his size, gnashed his teeth, rose on his hind legs and leant on the other who was doing the same. Like Cassius Clays they swayed about, clutched closely together, snapping at each other's snouts. They fell over, wrestled in a tight ball, arching their bodies and kicking with their hind feet. The round over, they paused to draw breath, one actually smoothing his fur and scratching his stomach, before resuming battle again. Meanwhile, the female nibbled some new green shoots among the tussocks of grass, her stub of a tail jauntily up. One male was winning! He was constantly on top, then threw the other with a kick. The weaker squeaked and threatened again, but he was ignored. Sheepishly he turned and ran, leaving the other two to mate.

"How many lemmings does a wolf need for a meal?" asked Bruce.

Myrtle Simpson and Rory
Devon Island camp. June
1969.

Arctic Fox. Devon Island,
July, 1969.

Old squaw duck (Rory's friend) at Cape Sparbo camp, Devon Island, N.W.T. July, 1969.

Black-bellied plover on Devon Island, N.W.T. July, 1969. (Taken with 20 cm telephoto.)

Ermine at Cape Sparbo, Devon Island. July, 1969.

"A dozen or two, I would say," I answered.

Hugh and Roger returned full of news. Everything was happening at once. On every stroll from the tent we found new treasures. Below our camp a meadow was appearing. Under the vegetation permafrost prevented the thawing snow from draining away. Miniature lochans formed, and meandering streams. The children were enchanted, finding new excitements at every turn.

Rona skipped up to the tent, purple flowers in her hair. "They're growing all over the beach," she said. The lethargy and weariness from our polar trip had fallen away from me. I groped under a pile of anoraks and nappies for the flower press. It belonged to the Edinburgh Botanic Gardens. I had collected for them in Greenland and Spitzbergen and the Curator had been delighted when I offered to press the flowers growing at this latitude in the Canadian Archipelago.

I found the boys down on the beach, lying on their stomachs, munching. They were eating the flowers!

"The Eskimos ate these at Resolute," they said indignantly. "Didn't you know the purple saxifrage is full of Vitamin C?"

Rory was sitting on a tussock of grey lichen, a thoughtful expression on his face. He was turning something over with his tongue, moving it from cheek to cheek. Delighted to show me, he opened his mouth. A large furry caterpillar fell out, russet, with a strip of bright orange down each side. Rory picked it up between two fingers and popped it in his mouth again.

"He doesn't eat it," explained Rona, who seemed to know. "He just likes the feel of it on his tongue. If I give him a cater-pillar he stays in one place and doesn't trouble me. I'm being a princess." She stretched her arms and pirouetted on the grey moss in the sun, her daisy chain of purple saxifrage sparkling in her golden hair. A flight of snow buntings rose and fell against the sky, like black and white butterfles.

Stirring the surface of the lagoon between the shore and the ice was a chestnut miniature gull, a broad white strip on each cheek. It floated buoyantly like a cork, and, very busily, it was twisting and turning round and round, stirring up the insects and larvae lying at the bottom of the water, popping its head down daintily to catch the morsels with its yellow beak. It was my favourite bird—a grey phalarope. Farther off, was the dowdier, cinnamon-toned male. He was uttering a cooing "pree-ree-reet". She answered with a quick twitter, then, as if remembering that she did want eggs after all, she lapsed into a soft, melodious "buu-ee, buu-ee". He swam towards her, aimlessly, constantly changing course, nodding his head and dipping his bill. He stuck to the shallow water, swimming near to the shore and following all indentations of the banks. Meanwhile, she was gyrating on one spot of the surface, anti-clockwise, as if tied to a pivot.

The phalarope completely ignored us. As the male approached, the female rose on the surface to an almost vertical position, with her head bent forward, and flapped her wings with a whirring sound, then flew aggressively at the male. He retreated to a boggy, sedgy place, below our camp. She followed, danced on her brownish lobed feet in front of him, ran into the sedge, watched him scratch a place for a suggested nest, rejected it, selected a spot herself, which he inspected.

"Oh, love again," said Bruce in a bored voice, who was watching by my side.

"Build a little cairn so that we can find the place again." I told him. "They will nest near here, and lay four buffish, spotty eggs by the middle of the month. Then, it's the male that sits on them, and defends the nest till the chicks can swim."

"Look at this," said Hugh indignantly as we returned to the tent. He held a tiny bundle of squeaking fur in his hand, its cheeks bulging with shreds of black plastic. "The bloody lemmings have got at my test tube covers. They've worn a patch right up to and under the tent. They're carting them off."

"They only want them for their nest. Surely you can spare a few."

"A few," exclaimed Hugh, "they've already got about a hundred or so, and I've only got twenty-two left."

As I was strolling off by myself one day searching for plants, a huge bird glided over my head, nonchalantly nearly sweeping my face with its wings. It landed and fixed me with one beady eye. Without dislocating its neck, it completely rotated its head and glowered at me with the other eye. It opened its huge beak and said, unmistakably "too-wit, too-woo". A snowy owl. In a flash of movement it was off.

"Go away, go away," I heard Rona shout. She was crouching in the snow, with her arms above her head and was thrashing at a mass of moving white feathers. "It's eating my lemmings," she screamed, attempting to cover several at once. The owl refused to be agitated. Disdainfully, it rose high in the air, a limp furry body sagging out of its beak. It flew towards the sea, then veered towards Cape Sparbo.

Where did it nest? I spent hours searching for a snowy owl's retreat in Greenland, with no success.

"Let's go and find it," I urged the others, over our supper in the tent. "The sea ice will be gone soon, and then we will not be able to travel over the bay. Come on, Hugh. I'm going anyway. I've been static long enough."

I succeeded in firing the others with my enthusiasm.

Taking enough food for two days and the little tent, we all set off early the next day. It was easy going at first, down towards the sea, then gingerly we lifted our skis over the tide crack. It was a foot wide. I tried not to look down but my attention was caught by a crayfish grovelling about in the open water. This bay ice moved about with the rise and fall of the tide. To my surprise Rona stepped over the gap without turning a hair. She was maddeningly unpredictable—as likely to be the feeble maiden as a big time explorer. Hugh then led our little team away from the shore. He was carrying his scientific gear in a large white box on his pack frame. We were not to be allowed time off. Roger was loaded with the billy-can, cameras and gun. Robin carried the tent, Bruce some dehydrated food in his tartan rucksack, Rona the Primus lashed round her neck and me, Rory. I had wrapped him up with the big double sleeping-bag, like a jam sponge, before stuffing him into his carry seat. Although the sun glittered down on us, a freezing wind was lashing across the ice over Jones Sound between Devon and Ellesmere Islands.

The pressure of the tide had cracked the ice and thrown great slabs of it about like confetti. I felt at home and skied confidently out into the Sound calling to the children to keep close. Rory was already fast asleep, snoring on my back. Oh,

it was great to be alive. The mountains of Ellesmere were
etched on the horizon hanging above the ice with the mirage
effect of cold air currents above the warm land. I lifted my face
'to the sun and felt it in my pores. I thought I would never
satisfy my thirst for the sun. The snow crystals split the rays of
it and sparkled jewels into my eyes. The surface of the snow
was soggy as the June sun beat down out of the crystal sky.
There was no monotony—each block of ice was a new sculpture,
its form changing as we drew up and passed it by, and threaded
away round to the next.

"Somebody's been here before," piped Rona. Her face was
scarlet from her efforts to keep up, the black fur of her anorak
hood framing her hair, which reflected the sun in a cascade of
golden light. She pointed with her ski stick to an enormous
footprint right across our path.

Polar bears. Water was collecting in the impression. Those
big feet with the five outstretched claws had plodded along very,
very recently! I glanced about. I remembered that a bear stalks
its prey silently. Hugh and Roger, I now realised, had drawn
ahead. Full of *joie de vivre* they were outdoing each other with
speed. If I called to them who would hear me first? Hugh or the
bear? It must be somewhere close by. I said nothing and urged
the children on. Robin and Bruce set off at speed using the long
Norwegian stride of the cross-country skier.

"I need a pee," announced Rona, undoing her skis.

"You can't," I answered, exasperated.

"I've got to," she said. Infuriatingly slowly, she peeled off
three pairs of trousers; one boot came off as well. I submerged
my mounting panic by bellowing at her like a fishwife.

"Why are you frightened?" she asked, crouching down.
"Mum, it's lovely here."

Looking about I appreciated that bear tracks were everywhere, big pad imprints as well as tiny ones. We must be in a
denning area, I realised, horrified. At last we set off once more.
We followed the others' tracks round the blind corners, my
heart in my mouth.

"Mum!" screamed Rona. "Look!" I jerked round seeing
nothing. "Rory's hat's over his eyes. He'll suffocate."

I wanted to bonk her with my ski stick. Why ever did I bring

Rona, I thought, as she dropped behind again. Is it true that the dangers which make adventures are the inventions of people who need to spice their existence with them to fill a void? Perhaps for an adult, but not for a child; they accept reality for what it is, matter-of-factly and calmly observing and registering facts. Their imagination works on the familiar and known. On the new and strange they are realists.

"Where does the bear have her babies?" Rona asked me now.

I explained that the she-bear gives birth in December in a hibernating den which she builds in a snow bank. When the cubs begin to walk out the mother bear is at her most aggressive and also her hungriest.

Eventually we caught up with the others who were leaning against an ice block munching chocolate.

"What kept you?" said Hugh. "There are bears about you know."

The ice was now swaying beneath our skis and the slush on the surface was becoming deeper.

"When's Jones Noise going to sink?" asked Rona.

"Jones Sound, you idiot," answered Robin, his round face glowing with enthusiasm for the journey. "Come on, let's go."

Our landfall was drawing near. Would we find a place to cross the tide crack, I wondered as we headed for a little indentation in the cliffs. A firm ice block made a tottering bridge and we filed across, safe again. I could see purple splashes of saxifrage on the brown-grey shingle exposed between the bay ice and the beach. I threw myself down on the flowers, feeling the texture of petal and leaf. Two tossing heads of yellow arctic poppy were growing out of a crack in a rock. They looked too delicate for here and reminded me of cornfields and cows. We pitched the tent on grass. Spring had come early to this little bay, with its secret glen winding up between the cliffs behind.

The children were ranging the slopes.

"I've found a whale," shouted Robin from a little col two hundred feet above. "How did it get up here?"

"Well, it didn't walk, anyway," answered Roger. "That shows where the sea came once."

When had shrill voices been heard here last, I wondered. I had a feeling that the Eskimos weren't really dead, but only dormant under the permafrost. I often felt another person at my side in the Arctic, as did Scott in the Antarctic. Polar regions in fact, seem to lend themselves to extrasensory perception.

A swoosh of many wings brought me into the present. Out of the sky swept a skein of geese. The sound of their wings lay in the air after the birds had passed. They were pure white, but for pitch-black tips to their greater primary feathers: snow geese. They had come from the Great Lakes and the lush green of southern U.S.A., looking for a tranquil place to lay their large greenish eggs. They landed untidily, but collected themselves and walked with great dignity up and down a green sward. They stretched themselves before arching their beautiful necks, and thrusting their bills about searching for something to eat. The white of their bodies was thrown against the sombre grey of the rocks. They called to each other in a mournful honk that echoed across the valley, to and fro, the sound bouncing from the rock wall above.

The boys were hiding behind a rock, playing at "Eskimo hunters". Real hunters caught geese with bolas, or killamittaun, made from bone weights tied to sinew strings, which were all joined together at one end. It was given a single twirl and thrown up into the midst of a flight of birds, where one or two would become entangled and fall to the ground. The hunter concealed himself in a position for a side "shot" at the geese (which like to fly against the wind, slowly), so there would be less chance of breaking the bolas strings.

Eskimo families used to set up camp along the coast, with goose-hunting as the objective. The only opportunity of catching a good quantity of the birds was during their flight north. If it looked as if the geese would bypass the hide, the Eskimo would try to lure them to him by imitating their call. Sometimes, previously killed birds were placed near the hide with their heads held up by sticks, to make lifelike decoys.

Rory was yelling for some food, so I ran back down the slope. "Bring some stones," shouted Hugh, "for the valance of the tent. This looks a windy place."

There were plenty of grey boulders about, blotches of black lichen on their side, weathered by years and years of storm and frost. I felt guilty as I turned one over, and so exposed a raw new side to the air. No one had ever moved them before. Why should I?

We all squashed into the one little tent. Life was simple again. Only one billy-can. No arguing as to the choice of rice or macaroni. We only had meat-bar stew.

In spite of the sun streaming through the thin walls of the tent, we were tired after the journey over the ice, and were soon fast asleep.

"Cosy up to me. I'm freezing," said Rona, waking me during the night. I pulled her inside our bag. The boys were so exhausted that I could actually bend their limbs so as to give me more room without them even stirring. Before going back to sleep, I looked out. Any sign of the snowy owl?

The silence of the Arctic night overawed me. No sound. No movement. The sun still shone high out of a cloudless blue sky, yet I knew it was night by the utter peace, as if the world were holding its breath. Eskimos have a story of the origin of the sun and moon. A girl—the sun—was playing a game of putting out the lights. She recognised her brother—the moon—and fled from him carrying a torch. Her brother chased her, but he only had time to half light his torch. They continue the chase to this day.

The snowy owl outwitted us. We found his cache of dead lemmings, and his favourite perch. We saw him constantly, but he never let us find his nest. We explored the glen right back to its source. A series of hanging valleys separated by steep walls of rock, led us higher and higher above the sea. As we gained altitude I felt that we were climbing back into time, retreating into the ice age that only recently had begun to relinquish its grip.

With Rory on my back, I travelled slowly and the boys scrambled easily ahead. I always had a clutch of red anoraks in front to show me the way that Hugh and Roger had taken up the rocks. They were great grey slabs at an angle of seventy degrees, but frost had split them, forming grooves and chimneys, ledges and gulleys, turning a severe climb into an easy scramble. Nothing compares to the satisfaction of picking a route up a wall of rock. I felt for a hold for my hands. Saw a place for my feet. Moved into it, shifted my weight, stood up and chose the next sequence without a pause. Above I could see the sun. The walls were opening out. We must be nearly up. I reached the others on a wide ledge.

Robin's face was radiant. "That was the real thing, Mum," he gasped with excitement. This was his Everest. In spite of the sun, the temperature was only plus 12. Hurriedly we climbed the last rocks. Above, a belt of muddy glacier-silt led back to the edge of the ice. It's greenness and looked evil uninviting: pre-historic, and dead. I wanted to get back down into the spring. The ice cap spreads right over this east end of Devon, and a traverse would have taken us to the south coast, and a view to Baffin Island and the north west passage.

"Too cold for the kids," I yelled at Hugh, the icy wind whipping my words away. We turned, and headed back for the tent, a microscopic dot below.

As we lost height, I noticed a white ball bowling up a steep snow bank, looking like a rubber toy. Back down it bounced, then up again. Then it changed into a tuft of cotton wool and was carried along by the wind, over the rocks and down and along the exposed stretch of beach. I hurried to loose height to see what it was. I was mesmerized by its graceful movements. Suddenly, it bounced towards us, and I realized that it was a fox.

Hugh motioned us to keep down. He could see that the fox was after a ptarmigan. The bird now waddled round a boulder into my vision. Its spring moult was on, and it looked tattered and torn, a mixture of yellow-brown spots on its back, and still its winter white feathers on its breast. Above its beady eye was a red, arched stripe. It froze, sensing danger and its colour completely conformed to the surroundings, the mottled feathers camouflaging with the lichen covered rocks.

Rona moved, the ptarmigan jerked its head, and noisily rose from the ground. It flew heavily with rapid wing beats and long glides, and stopped again fifty yards away. It now mounted a boulder and stood looking about, uttering a hoarse, guttural rattling note.

"It sounds like my fishing reel ticking out," whispered Robin.

"It's just a silly old hen," said Rona, standing up. "I'm hungry."

I remembered that Greenland Eskimo children stone ptarmigan then invariably tear out the intestines of the freshly killed bird and eat them raw while still warm, and with their content of half-digested green stuff. This is considered a delicacy and an excellent source of vitamins, and always handed first to the weakest child.

The fox was stalking warily nearer and nearer. Suddenly over our heads swooshed down the snowy owl! The fox jumped, yelping, the ptarmigan croaked and vanished, the owl flew straight up, feathers ruffled, looking outraged and we were left alone on the scene, with Rory crying loudly as his reaction to the drama.

"Lucky it wasn't a thunderbird," said Rona, "or it might have taken us! Pudluk saw one once, he told me, but the last one's gone now."

"I'll tell you the story," interrupted Bruce. "Rona will get it all wrong. You see, there was this boy Nahnuk, and he saw a great herd of reindeer coming near his village. Just as he was about to let go his walrus-ivory tipped arrow, an enormous thunderbird picked him up and carried him off. It flew higher and higher until Nahnuk couldn't see the earth. But he freed one arm from the claws, reached for his hunting knife he always carried in his belt and stabbed the bird. Twice. He got its heart, its blood flowed out and it got weaker and weaker and lower to the ground. It fell and Nahnuk watched while the huge bird died. Its feathers were beautiful and Nahnuk plucked out the largest and always carried it with him as a charm. It made him the best hunter in the village.

"One day a year later it was such a lovely day he rushed off to hunt and forgot his feather. He had just started off when another thunderbird swooped down and got him again. It said, 'Please don't kill me. My mother wants to see you.' Up and up soared the bird till Nahnuk couldn't see the earth. They flew till he heard a loud noise like drum beats. It came from a huge nest. The bird landed on it, and said, 'The noise you hear is my mother's heart beating for her other son you killed last year.'

"The noise was so loud that it frightened Nahnuk. The mother bird lay on a pile of soft furs. She said, 'My son wants his feathers. He cannot come to see me without them. You must burn them and at the same time you must set his heart beating again by dancing to a drum that sounds exactly like my heart.'

" 'I will,' said Nahnuk, and the thunderbird took him home.

"Nahnuk tried to find a drum that sounded like the mother's heart-beat. He tried wooden boats and skin kayaks and the missionary's tin buckets but none were right. Then he thought of lashing together two reindeer ribs and stretching the reindeer stomach across it. He beat the drum and it was exactly right!

"Nahnuk then started a fire. He danced round it, beating on the drum. When he was dancing madly, leaping in the air and hammering out the beats, he threw the feathers on to the flames. There was a great flash of light, and with a sound of thunder banging and crashing, a huge bird flew out of the flames and up into the sky.

"Thunderbirds have never troubled Eskimos since."

I thought of that pastoral scene of grazing geese as we skied back towards our base-camp next day. The sea ice was creaking and swaying in earnest now. The tide flooded over it, sometimes to a depth of two feet, and we slushed through water wet to the knees. The sun glared down, really hot, and we sweated under our windproofs.

Black lozenge-shaped seals lay humped on the ice. Immobile till we approached, then instantly gone, tumbling into their blow-hole, as they caught sight of our little party. Sometimes the larger bolder males waited until we could see into their immense dark eyes.

I thought of Scott's last expedition, when one of his subsidiary support parties was stranded during the winter by open water. They lived in an igloo and were desperately short of food as they had to save their sledge rations for the return journey. They lived off seal and penguin, but the open water made hunting difficult. Then came a red letter day! They did manage to catch a seal, and inside its stomach were thirty-six fish, undigested and very edible. After that, whenever a seal was sighted the party would shout "fish". The six men in their group ate seal blubber, cooked with seal blubber, used blubber lamps. Their clothes and gear became soaked with blubber, till the clothes stood up by themselves in spite of scraping;

and the soot from the lamps blackened their skin, their sleeping bags and cookers, and gave them constant red eyes and sore throats.

Freuchen too, was once in a similar position with one companion, Mala, the only survivor of a famine in an Eskimo camp. He was a young boy of about eight. On the fourth day without food, Mala shouted hysterically at Freuchen, "Don't look at me like that," and the big Dane realised that Mala's relations had turned cannibal as a last resort before they died of hunger.

Eventually Freuchen did shoot a seal. He and Mala rushed to it like madmen. They lapped up the blood streaming from the bullet hole, and stroked the skin, considering where to start eating.

They used the blubber for fuel by chewing the fat and spewing it out over some turf. Then they found two flat stones and sandwiched the meat between them, then roasted it on the fire.

Freuchen said the best meal he ever had in his life was when they reached the brain, and he laid half of it on a piece of blubber and chopped in blubber oil. "It was so delicious," he wrote years afterwards, "that the mere thought of it still excites my salivary glands."

What a contrast to our Arctic world, I thought, as we reached our base. Our main camp now seemed to have the luxuries of home. Dry fresh nappies, enough paraffin actually to heat a billy-can of water to waste on washing my face. I settled down inside now and opened my flower press and added the frail petals and leaves that I had found on our journey.

Hugh was as happy with his samples of urine. He sat in his observation tent surrounded by urine bottles and data sheets. While most of the results would have to await laboratory analysis in the U.K., some data could already be worked up: for example he was working out the average of our hand-grip strength for each day of the twenty-one-hour day cycle. This was important since our routine was in effect a static simulation of an eastward circumglobal flight, flying 45 degrees longitude per day. Thus grip strength on "day 1" of the cycle was like being at home on the Greenwich meridian while day 2 equalled West Russia, day 3 East Russia, and day 4 brought one past the date line etc. He was excited to find that as the cycle days 1–4 passed, the grip strength became weaker, then for days 5–8 it regained the initial strength. The effect was not great but the statistics showed that the probability was 1:100 that it was not chance alone. The mental acuity tests (adding random numbers) also showed slight but definite decrements of performance during the "out of phase periods".*

* see Appendix I

CHAPTER NINE

JUNE IS THE FLOWERING month in the high Arctic. By the beginning of the month a steadily increasing number of plant species burst into bloom. Vegetation is at its height of abundance and the tundra lands of Greenland, Alaska, Spitzbergen and Canada are lush and green. The entire development of the plants depends on moisture. Everywhere the ground is thawing and snow melting rapidly. On Devon Island, some of this water was rushing down from the heights in torrents, causing the rivers to flood and channels to carve into the sandy and shingly raised beach. But a fair amount of water was trapped, and this formed the main supply for the plants. By the end of the month they have another source of moisture: because the sun heats the land, cold winds blow in from the sea to fill the gap created by the rising hot air, and dense damp fog is formed; this creeps along the land, soaking everything and enveloping the plants in a blanket of moisture. They lap it up, converting it into new leaves and shoots.

The dull grey-green of Arctic willow predominates to make a compact mat with mingling splashes of rich green cassiope. White bell-flowers, like dew drops, rested on heathery stems, a contrast to the waxed, symmetrical flowers of the wintergreen, which grew in the most favoured spots beneath the rocks. The plants of the high Arctic are almost all characterised by their small size—their stunted growth and compact stature, in the form of cushions, rosettes and tufts, showing their resistance to wind and drifting snow as well as to drought. The leaves are small and often leathery and sometimes they are covered by densely matted hairs which serve to reduce evaporation. The poor soil and the severe climate even during the short growing months slow down the rate of growth and it often takes scores of years for a willow shrub to reach its maximum height of a few feet. Arctic plants show how little the requirements of life can be, and how the most difficult situations can be surmounted.

By the end of the month there were seed-pods among the blooms. Fragile negatives, like a floral art arrangement, wafted in the wind, particularly among the many varieties of Draba which are all members of the mustard family. As I walked along the rocky ledges, and across the marshes I very seldom found seedlings. They are very rare in the high arctic regions. Some flowers, like a number of grasses, saxifrages and butter-cups, never produce mature seeds at all and multiply exclusively by vegetation. This is perhaps due to the comparatively small number of arctic insects, and so the plants must be self-pollinat-ing in order to survive. Any flowers that do produce seeds do so in quantity, but the low summer temperatures make the soil so dry and cold, from midsummer on, that they do not germinate. The seeds must pass the winter, waiting until spring when the melting snow makes the soil sufficiently moist for germination, which is more important to them than the cold temperature. The most successful plants reproduce by sending out roots, by means of shoots or subterranean runners, or even by transformation of buds into bulbils which become detached from the mother plant when able to take up a life of their own.

By now already ninety-four different varieties of flowering plants were safely pressing inside my blotting paper. I was busy with these one morning when Rona interrupted me.

"There's a shaggy animal, like a blanket, coming down fast," she said looking into the tent.

"Oh, tell Dad," I answered, not wanting to be disturbed.

"He's gone off on the ice with Roger to try and take photos of a baby seal," she replied, in her high-pitched voice.

Reluctantly, I looked out, to find a musk ox completely filling my range of vision! It was covered in long brown hair, thickly matted and curly on the shoulders but elsewhere straight and hanging down. Its legs were stout and short. There are very few of these creatures alive in the world today, although they used to range over the plains of Germany and France, and traces have even been found by geologists in Pleistocene gravels in England. The size of a bison, the musk ox is really a relation of a sheep, but its huge downward curving horns, that meet on the same plane as its eye, can mean business, as I knew from being chased by one in Greenland! I had also crept up on a small herd in Spitzbergen, hoping to take photographs. They had taken exception to this and had driven me into a river. I had managed to reach a shingly island and there had to wait with nothing but my camera until rescue the next day. Musk ox usually wander about in herds, but a young or old male is sometimes ostracised by his wives and pushed out.

This one, looking at me, stood five feet on the shoulders and appeared indignant at our infringement of its territorial rights. Obviously it was moving up the coast of Devon and had reached the area of our camp while we were away looking for the snowy owl's nest.

Rory, catching sight of the animal, shrieked with delight. At this the musk ox hesitated, snorted, pawed the ground uncertainly then ambled off, lifting its woolly legs like a highland bull.

"Look what it's left behind," cried Rona, picking handfuls of soft wool from the ground in each of the animal's vast cloven hoof prints, that did him for snow shoes in the winter. Eskimos collected this discarded winter coat and stuffed it into their sealskin mitts and kamiks. They said it absorbed the sweat and was far warmer than any other form of wool. It was also prized for swaddling clothes for a new-born child, and was as soft and light as down.

"Where are the boys?" I asked Rona.

"I don't know," she said. "They told me they were off for a swim," she added nonchalantly. "They might have gone towards Robin's snow bunting nest."

I allowed the boys to range far over the rocks that now encircled our camp. Only a few banks of snow remained, in deep fissures on shadowy sides of the outcrops. Heavens, I thought, whatever will they do if they see this musk ox, or what will it do if it sees them first? I hoisted Rory on to my shoulders and rushed out of the tent, remembering just in time to turn off the Primus. A wispy fog lay low on the ground masking the sun as if with tissue paper. The mist silenced the birds, even Rona's shrill voice was subdued.

"The world's gone small," she said running after me.

I loved the feel of the rocks as I strode over them. Their roughened slabs gave ample hold to my boots. Mini-gardens nestled in cracks and crannies, a jigsaw of green on the grey.

"Oh, look!" shouted Rona, kneeling down suddenly. "Here's one you haven't got."

Her quick eyes had spotted a tiny dense cluster of white flowers sparkling out from the tops of a long stalk. The dark green, nearly purplish leaves were oval-shaped and saw-edged.

"It's saxifrage nevalis," I said, excited, as if we had found a diamond. I lifted Rory down and dug in my pocket for my knife.

"Where's that flower?" I said, puzzled, as I crouched down.

"Oh, you bad Rory," screeched Rona. "You've eaten it!"

Wanting to oblige, Rory spat out a mouthful of green into my hand, the odd wet petal, proving she was right.

"Never mind. There's another one," I said with relief, hastily putting it into my box.

Through the mist I could sense the sea. The rise and fall of the tide had by now formed a broad stretch of water between the land and the ice. A slight breeze stirred the mist and I caught sight of two pink bodies gleaming wet in the muffled sunlight. The boys were bathing! Quite oblivious to us, they were pottering about in the water.

"Give me a hand up," shouted Bruce to Robin. "I can't get my foot up on to the ice ledge."

Four male common eider ducks were watching them, cooing conversationally to each other as they drifted along in the breeze. The drakes had changed their beautiful contrasting colour pattern of the mating season for a modest drab garb similar to the females. The reason for this "eclipse" dress is because the drakes renew their flight feathers and during this period are unable to fly. So they try to conceal themselves and withdraw to secluded places in retreat.

"Croo, croo," murmured Rory to the ducks, in exact imitation of the tone. Though unable to talk to us, he got on famously with the birds and bees.

"It's great, Mum, come on in," shouted Robin, catching sight of us. "It's not cold at all if you don't keep your feet on the ice for long."

Musk ox at Cape Sparbo, Devon Island, N.W.T.

Rory finds the remains of a musk ox left by wolves the previous winter. Devon Island, July, 1969.

Rona, Robin and Bruce sleeping out on Devon Island, July, 1969. Their bed is within a stone circle put up by the whalebone culture Eskimos some centuries back.

His dark curly head submerged with a splash and the ducks bobbed up and down, disturbed by the ripples.

"There's hairy monsters about," shouted Rona, peeling off her pants. "Wait for me."

Already I was cold from standing watching. I wandered up the beach to a largish black rock. As I approached it moved off! The musk ox again. I looked closer at the other rocks about me. Some were in tidy piles, leaning together like a card house, a flat stone on the bottom. Someone had built this, and I recognised an Eskimo cache. Eider ducks were an important source of food in the old days. The females lay their eggs and prepare their nests in the middle of June. The mother duck must keep the nest warm and have sufficient strength to stand the long period of fasting involved, and so she is very fat at this time. The Eskimos liked to go after the succulent females, and took the males only to eat at once, but kept the others for later consumption. They considered a fusty duck the most appetising dish one could serve for special guests! They stored them by building a little tower of stone and hanging them up by their bills so that they did not reach the ground. Flat stones were placed between them to keep them from touching each other. The stone on the floor prevented the birds from coming in contact with the grass or moss which would spoil them, owing to the moisture from the ground. Such cached ducks are called "igunaq", and must always be protected from the sun. If stored properly they will last to the following winter when they are brought home to be eaten as a delicacy. If such female ducks have an egg or two inside, the yolk turns black and tastes like blue cheese and is prized even more.

The proper way to cook a female duck is to pluck off all the feathers and down, then skin the bird to the neck. The meat is added to a boiling pot, but the skin is tied round the neck to form a closed bag which is dropped in the boiling water. The fat inside the skin melts and the skin bag itself swells so that it looks as if it were stuffed to capacity. When it is finished, the cook opens it by unwrapping the string round the neck, releasing the liquid fat, which pours out. Children and best friends are invited to get some of the hot fat by sucking it straight from the skin through the neck, and when the skin is entirely emptied, it and the meat are eaten with great relish. Another traditional delicacy was the egg sausage, for which the Eskimo wife needed about a hundred fresh eiders' eggs. This was usually a job for the old women. They cracked the eggs in such a way that they were able to suck out the white which was at once spat on the ground, as only the yolk was needed. This the old women also sucked out of the shell but they then spat it carefully into the dried intestine of a seal. It was essential that no white went with the yolk as this would spoil the finished product. If the smallest bit of albumen did get into the sausage, it could be seen from outside and a small hole was made to extract it. Then the butt end of a feather was put in, as a cork, to stop the leak in the intestine. After the sausage was filled it was dried by hanging in the open air. Sometimes it took the entire summer and had to be carefully watched so that the sun did not shine directly on it and so turn it rancid. When it was thoroughly dried it was cut up into small pieces, and eaten like tablet or fudge.

There were other signs of Eskimo life about me as I stood on the beach, waiting for the children: a circle of stones that had kept down a summer tent; pieces of whalebone that had formed a roof to a proper house. The Eskimos of Devon Island had belonged to the Thule culture; they settled on this coast perhaps ten centuries ago, their economy based on the hunting of the Greenland whale. This large animal provided a good deal of what was essential to life: oil for their lamps, food, and bone for use in the construction of their houses. About the beginning of the eighteenth-century conditions changed. The climate became colder and the narrow waters of the inland seas, full with ice at the best of times, now remained frozen throughout the short summer. This restricted the passage of the grey whales and, coupled with the massacre by the European whaling ships, fewer of these animals reached the high Arctic. The people of the Thule culture were forced to abandon their villages, break up into small groups and change their way of life to hunting reindeer, seal and walrus. The weathered bones that once formed the walls and roofs of their dwellings stuck out around me from the tundra, like ribs from an open grave. In some places the turfs that had formed the roof had now grown back into the ground, leaving a cave underneath. I looked into one of these. Instead of anthropological remains there were some pieces of Cadbury's chocolate. My children had been playing house. Fragments of soapstone acted as plates, and shreds of bone for knives. One that I handled had been formed into an arrow head with a smooth apex and an open socket on each side. The dwelling was below ground level, with one slab of rock forming a deck across a third of the floor. This would have been the family sleeping shelf. Nansen described an encounter with people living in houses like this when he landed on the east coast of Greenland in 1884. He described them as a strangely wild and shaggy looking lot, all dressed in furs, who stared and pointed at him uttering a bovine sound which Nansen said was as if he had a whole herd of cows about him, lowing in chorus as the cow-house door was opened in the morning to admit the expected food. The Eskimos gave him a great welcome and the men rushed forward to show him a good landing place for his boat. He met beaming smiles on all sides and appreciated that this was the Eskimos' greeting to a stranger as their language had no formula for welcome. Nansen related that these people seemed to be comfortable enough in their home amid the ice and rocks. An enticing glow shone out of their communal dwelling and he was at once invited in by signs. He accepted the invitation and as soon as he had passed the doorway a curtain of thin membraneous skin was pushed aside and he bent his head to enter, and found himself in a cosy room. Nansen's attention was then fully occupied by the smell! Oil lamps were burning and their powerful odour, said Nansen, "was well tempered with human exhalations of every conceivable kind as well as the pungent effluvia of a certain fetid liquid which was stored in vessels here and there about the room and which, as I subsequently learned, is, from the various uses to which it is applied, one of the most important and valuable commodities of Eskimo domestic economy." In other words, the Eskimos collected urine as enthusiastically as Hugh! Nansen's Eskimos had their fire in a hollow on the ground floor which kept the temperature at body level consistent. Eskimo families slept on the sleeping shelf, all piling in together to keep warm.

"What are you doing with my things?" said Rona, indignantly, coming up to me. "That's my Wendy House you
know."

We wandered slowly back towards our camp through the
mist. The moisture sat in droplets on the leaves of the plants,
trapped in the tiny hairs. Rona pointed at one flower, looking like
a tinselled decoration, shimmering out of the flat background.

"I wish you had called me by that's name," she said, longingly. The rich yellow potentilla nestled on its silvery leaves
growing low against the rock, in a dry and sandy crevasse.

Suddenly we stopped in our tracks; even the children silenced.
Out of the mist walked a man! A bulky duffel jacket hid his
shape, a huge rucksack sat on his back and a gun was slung
at the ready by his side. We gulped at him, feeling like one of
Nansen's Eskimos.

"Hi!" he said. "I am from the Arctic Institute of North
America. I am on an expedition to gather material for my
PhD. thesis."

"An expedition?" I interrupted. "Where are you going?"

"Going?" he said. "I'm here already. My expedition is to
Devon Island."

"Oh," said Rona. "We're just here for our holidays."

"What are you hunting for?" asked Robin enthusiastically,
already fingering the scientist's gun.

He had not put on his clothes properly after his swim and
was carrying his socks and boots.

"It's for protection," replied the scientist. "It's dangerous
here. We never leave the hut without a gun."

He looked apprehensively over his shoulder as if expecting a
tiger to jump out of the mist. The scientist accompanied us back
to the camp and Hugh took over the conversation on a higher
scientific plane.

"You mean to say you can pursue a research project from
that old tent," said our visitor after Hugh had talked to him for
about an hour.

"Sit down and have a cup of coffee," I said hospitably
proferring a grimy plastic mug.

"No thank you. I don't drink coffee—or tea, or cocoa," he
added hastily, glancing over at our provisions, stacked on the

Robin being bathed by Mum while Rory plays with his favourite toy—an emergency whistle in case of polar bear visits.

Cape Sparbo camp, Devon Island, N.W.T. July, 1969. Myrtle, Rory, and Robin cleaning a seal-skin.

ground. Meanwhile the scientist laid down an oblong perspex box he had been carrying, in order to read Hugh's pro forma on rhythms. He read it as if scrutinising our credentials.

Rory's fingers itched to fiddle. I watched him push past the other children, who were mesmerised by the visitor, and he lifted the box belonging to the scientist. However, I presumed the lid was serviceable, and turned away to measure out some yeast. Roger made the best bread, baking it slowly over the Primus in a box oven. Hugh was the expert on rolls. He insisted that the crusts must be brick-like, although we tried hard to get the message through that we much preferred them soft.

"Do you have ski-doos?" inquired the scientist, "and how often do you get a re-supply by plane?"

"We have neither," answered Hugh. "We travel on foot."

"Oh," said the scientist in a tone that made me feel a penniless migrant again.

He prepared to leave. "Oh," he repeated in anguish, "My specimens!"

I hastily glanced at Rory. He was chewing. I frantically gestured to the other children to keep quiet.

"What are you waving at me for?" asked Robin, maddeningly smug. "Rory's eaten them," he told the scientist. "He always does that. It's your fault; you shouldn't have left anything valuable on the ground."

Hugh soothed him diplomatically and the scientist returned to his hut, to complete his schedule for the day.

The following day I wandered off along the shore to collect plants. My eye was caught by a flicker of movement under a big rock.

"Tssisk—tssisk," "tssisk—tssisk," I heard. A small aristocratic weasel-like head appeared from the ledge below the big rock, an etching of white above cinnamon coloured ears. It was an ermine! Its long lithe body darted at speed over that rock, disappeared and popped out again a few feet farther on. A number of brownish heads with wrinkled noses and shiny black eyes appeared, vanished, reappeared somewhere else. The area seemed infested! In the light it was not easy to tell which were the young and which the parents, as the young were fluffy and looked larger than they were, while the female in any case was smaller than the yellower male. He had the loudest, crossest, voice, and indignantly cursed his children as they scampered to and fro. I put my hand in my pocket and tossed crumbs of dehydrated meat towards the rock. The darting movements converged on the desiccated meat. The six young pushed and shoved Dad out of the way. They looked as sharp as shrews. Now they frolicked and joyfully played, chasing one another up and down the rocks, biting each other's fur, spitting and grinding their teeth, practising at being grown up.

They caught sight of Mother now, a tiny scrawny chick in her jaws. They ran off to meet her, throwing themselves at her, tearing at it, squabbling for the tiny shreds of meat. The mother gave it to them, then stood and watched, seeing everything.

I crept away to tell the others of my discovery of the ermines' hide. As I jumped over the rocks towards our camp I came upon Robin, sobbing, his fat cheerful face distorted in misery. I put my arms around him and he wept uncontrollably on my neck.

"What is it?" I said at last, shaking him frantically, to get through to some sense.

"My nest's robbed. Two babies are dead, one's gone. Oh Mum, they were sweet and happy and their feathers were coming and now they're dead."

"I will show you what has got them," I said drawing him back after me towards the big rock.

The baby ermines were tumbling about in the snow. Robin's harrowed face smiled, as he watched the tiny devils chase each other at breakneck speed over and under and through the rocks, darting out here and popping out there, constantly moving and whipping about.

"I want to kill them," whispered Robin, loudly in my ear, "but I love them too. Why did they have to eat my chicks? It was my favourite snow bunting's nest." He began to sob again, clenched his fists, and kicked at the rocks in frustration. A cheeky ermine bobbed up on top of the rock, and cocked its head at the boy. It captured his attention, jumped down, and scampered over his foot. Robin crouched, enchanted now, and all the ermines boldly leapt into his hands and out, under his legs and over his arms. He rolled on his back, laughing, with the animals playing hide-and-seek over and under him.

CHAPTER TEN

JULY WAS OUR summer. A mother eider led a brood of young ducklings past our camp and on to our private lake. One fat pile of black fluff jumped on her back for a hitch then fell off and joined the others in line. Already some birds were leaving their breeding areas and moving south. After the middle of the month a decrease in the animal life of the land and lakes could be felt. The adult birds had left the available food supply to their young who had not yet finished their development. The earliest migrants were the shore birds and we heard their musical, haunting, reed-pipe noise in the evenings as they gathered and flew south. The phalaropes, turnstones, ringed plovers and dunlins had left us by the end of the month.

The tundra was quieter now as we roamed away from our camp, but the seashore was noisier than ever. Pirate skuas harassed the terns, pursuing the lither bird closely in the air with relentless tenacity, in order to steal its food. The delicate tern always tried bravely to escape by aerial gymnastics, but was always frustrated and disgorged its food for the fat skua.

Fat busy bumble-bees reminded us that it was high summer. They were large and rough, their plump bodies had dense hairy covering, well adapted to conserve the heat generated by the rapid vibrations of their wings. I lay in the sun on a bank of dark green dryas, squashing a few of the pale yellow wide open-faced flowers still lifting their delicate heads to the sun. Suddenly a blood curdling yowl seared through the air. I leapt to my feet. It was a child in agony, but I could see my four children contentedly playing "chuck stanes" at the edge of the lake. The shriek came again. It was the most ghastly sound I had ever heard, weird and horrible. It was answered by a long drawn out "oo-ee", more mournful and eerie, that shivered my spine.

Out on the lake I could see the dark silhouette of two Arctic loons, or red-necked divers, as we would call them at home; the head of one was raised to the sky, long black bill protruding.

between them circled two young. Could that beautiful bird really have made that dreadful noise? Something had alarmed them, I realised. Just at that moment I caught sight of a figure hurrying towards us across the tundra from the direction of the Arctic Institute hut. It was our scientist again. I got up slowly and walked towards him. He looked agitated and as I drew nearer he started to speak.

"One of our party is ill and he's stuck on the icecap. Any suggestions? The helicopter cannot fly in to pick him off because the summer thaw is melting the surface and the plane cannot land."

"Oh," I said. "What a pity, but I suppose they could walk down quite easily. The distance cannot be very far. It would only need a two or three day's trip."

"No," he said, "they have already tried once. They have no lightweight tent, only ski-doos and they cannot drive through the thaw."

Suddenly I realised the irony of the situation. We could travel lightly. We could walk over an icecap because we carried old-fashioned equipment and were not dependent on planes, radios, ski-doos and airlifts.

"Well," I said to him. "Perhaps we could go and bring them down."

"Yes, yes," he answered. "I hoped you were going to suggest that."

"Well," I said, "we had better go back and talk it over with Hugh and Rog."

Hugh asked medical questions. "What is the matter with him? What sort of pain has he got? How bad is it?"

"He has used up all their analgesics," said the scientist, "and he's already nearly drowned himself by trying to move half a mile away from their camp. It's a difficult situation."

"Well," said Roger, he and Hugh rising to the challenge, "I think we could make it. We will set off tomorrow morning with our light tent and a couple of day's food. Don't worry, we'll get him safely off and down to your base."

"Oh," said the scientist, "I must rush back to keep my schedule. Thanks a lot."

He looked cross at being interrupted at all from his scientific

project. Hugh shrugged his shoulders. There was no question
in his mind which got the priority; sick man or scientific
research undertaking.

Hugh and Roger walked off into the mist the following day,
their skis strapped on their shoulders and a few days' food in a
light pack. I was left alone with the children.

The tundra seemed empty and I felt sad. For the first time I
began to long for the comforts of home. I would not mind a bath,
I thought, and how marvellous to go to the theatre, or even
turn on the wireless, or just have a gossipy conversation over a
cup of coffee with a friend in the morning.

"Come, Mum. Robin's found something marvellous," said
Rona, tugging at my sleeve.

Rather reluctantly I followed her to where I could see the
boys crouched in the marshiest place in our surroundings. The
cold water oozed inside my boots. The temperatures were
now around forty, but at night it fell to well below freezing.
Robin was cradling something in his hands, a furious mother was
flapping her wings a little way off. She had a black splodge on
her stomach and stood on two longish legs, making the unmistakable call of the plover.

"Oh, look at this darling chick," said Robin and in his
hands lay a bundle of yellow fluff, its frantically beating heart
disturbing the down on its chest. Reluctantly, Robin let it go
and it lifted its long legs boldly out of the bog as it hurried
towards its mother.

"I want to show you something else," said Bruce. "One of
the wolves has got the musk ox."

Very surprised I followed them, on the higher ground where
the rocks were steeper and blacker, to a little lochan with mossy
banks and a few purple heads of figwort among the tossing tufts
of bog cotton which surrounded it. A heap of bones lay a few
feet away from the water. Hundreds of wolves' droppings were
piled up all around. The wolves had got it all right, I thought,
but not this year; probably the previous winter.

"Look at all the fur," said Rona, "there's enough to make us
all a jersey and Dad at least two."

In great excitement she was gathering armfuls and armfuls of
soft, chocolate-coloured musk ox wool.

F

"Get a sleeping bag," she shouted to the boys. "Quick, quick. Let's get it all and take it home."

Living off the land had by now become automatic, so I helped the children glean in the wool. This kept us busy that day and the next too. I constantly walked to the top of the rocks that gave us the longest view towards the icecap. No sign of the boys. The mist was thicker, all the time narrowing our horizon till it was a grey pall directly outside the tent and even filtered through, making our life a haze.

"I can't see the chess men properly," said Robin that evening waving the atmosphere with his hands.

"There's nothing for it but to go to bed," I said.

"Let's all sleep together then," said Rona. "I feel frightened with all this smoke."

We cuddled down together, all of us like a huddle of rabbits, and the night soon passed.

I was woken by a sound we had not yet heard on Devon Island—rain, hammering on the canvas. I knew the noise well from camping at home. Lashing rain was beating down on the Arctic snow.

"Gosh," said Robin. "It's just like Glencoe!"

"Look at it," said Bruce. "It's going to drown the lemmings and the ermines too, and the birds. Whatever will they do? Lucky their eggs have all hatched or else they would be washed out of the nests."

"Yes," I said, wondering just how many of the eggs did in fact survive, and the chicks fly south. There seemed more predators around than if the parent birds had stayed at home and nested in a cherry tree.

The weather grew worse all that day and the next. I began to worry about Hugh and Roger. With the summer's melt at this height water would be cascading off the icecap without all this rain adding to it. The rivers would be in spate and I remembered the story of the ill scientist nearly drowning in a melt stream. Heavens, I thought, the streams would be fifty times as big now. Water on ice is a dangerous thing. It carves a deep channel and there is no gravel on the bottom to cause friction and hold up the rate of flow; the water rushes along at breakneck speed. Climbing boots, even with crampons attached, behave like roller skates and one is instantly swept off one's feet.

We whiled away the day playing chess, drawing and redrawing on the same pieces of paper. I reopened our school and the children gave the next morning to learning a poem.

"The tide rises and the tide falls," intoned Rona.

"Twilight darkens, the curlew calls.

Along the sea sands damp and brown,

The traveller hastens towards the town.

The tide rises, the tide falls."

The words seemed to capture the mournfulness of our desolate scene. The sun was hanging significantly lower in the southern sky each day and it was growing darker very quickly, indicating that the seasons were turning and winter was not so very far away.

"I can hear Dad," said Bruce lifting his head and cocking his face on one side.

"Ooh-oo, ooh-oo."

Very faintly I could hear his call. Oblivious of the rain, we ran out of the tent. I snatched up Rory who was outside already and we ran up over the rocks to meet the two men.

They looked harrowed and hungry and so they might, as they had now been away for five days.

"What happened?" I said. "I thought you were drowned."

"Nothing happened," said Roger. "We got him off all right but the weather was foul."

"What was wrong?" I interrupted. "Did he have appendicitis or something worse?"

"Terrible," said Roger. "He had toothache."

"What?" I said aghast, thinking of what the boys had gone through during the last few days.

"Yes," said Roger. "He was warned that his tooth needed attention but hoped to make enough money on this summer's trip to pay the dentist's bills. I'm going to stop complaining about the National Health."

We walked back into the tent, as wet inside now as out.

"Wah! Where's the bread?" said Hugh. "I'm ravenous."

"Oh," I said, "There isn't any." I had to admit that I had been too dejected during the past few days to make it.

"What?" said Hugh, not understanding the effect of the

weather on my mind. "No bread? Whatever's wrong? We have only got two or three more days here, you know, before the plane comes."

"Don't be stupid," I replied. "It's only the third week in August."

"You're three weeks wrong," said Roger, "and the scientists are coming tomorrow to help us move camp up to their runway."

"Yes, better get cracking," said Hugh rushing towards his medical research tent in a fever of activity. "I must get these results finished. Come on. I'll need everyone's help."

Suddenly I felt sad. A few hours before, I was longing to relinquish this ice island for the comforts of home. Now I was as reluctant to go back. I remembered Nansen who had carefully missed the last boat out of Greenland back to Copenhagen because he could not bear to give up the lands of the north.

Rona began to cry. "I don't want to go," she said. "I can't leave my lemmings or that duck or those darling ermines and there's several snow bunting who haven't gone yet and I certainly *don't* want to go back to school."

"Oh," said Bruce. "I'm longing for a game of football in the playground."

"I'd love a bath," said Robin unexpectedly.

That reminded me. I stood up and lifted down the zinc tub used only for mixing the bread. We wouldn't need it any more now. I started to fill all available billy-cans with water and pumped the Primus up to "full". One by one I pulled the clothes off the children and poured hot water over their arms and legs. We had a little soap still and I was very surprised that this proved the children to be pink underneath their layer of grime. Rory screamed as I stretched out for him.

"He doesn't know about baths," explained Rona. "He just hated them in Resolute too."

Just then the scientists appeared.

"We're not ready," I said. "Hugh told me you were not coming till tomorrow."

"But it's 9 a.m. already," they answered, perplexed.

"You dolt," said Hugh. "They're on different time. Remember?"

I had forgotten that we had been living on Hugh's artificial length of day. Hastily now we began to pull things together. Bruce was rushing across the beach dragging back armfuls of treasures.

"You can't take all those you know," said Roger. "It's a £1 a pound excess baggage in the plane."

"I've got to take it," said Bruce. "It's my favourite bit of whalebone."

I reminded the children of dolls and train-sets at home, but they were not interested. Their most prized possessions were the treasures they had collected from our barren surroundings. It took us all day to move camp and only then did I realise that fog had set in once more. Obviously no plane could get through to collect us until it moved. I was glad. I was not mentally attuned to be whisked out of our surroundings back to civilisation. Already the world seemed too highly populated, with the scientists a stone's throw away in their hut.

"I'm going for a walk," I said to the others. "The children are fast asleep, tired out, and I have never got to the head of that glen. It's stopped raining now. Come on with me. You can sleep all the way home in the plane."

With difficulty I persuaded Hugh and Roger to join me and we crept away from the sleeping children. It was 1 a.m. Quickly we strode over the tundra away from the shore, up towards the head of the long glen to the west of the huts. The grass was yellowing already. The world was silent, waiting for the winter. We covered the ground at speed. We were as fit as we had ever been, after our months of living rough. The going was easy and we were soon high up among the outcrops of rock below the escarpment that led up to the ice-cap.

"Look," said Roger pointing towards six black boulders, but I knew them now to be musk ox. My eyes were attuned to the movements of the tundra and I knew what was what. We sat down to watch them, but soon another animal walked into our line of vision. It was a lone wolf. He was big, well-fed and white. In complete command of his environment he strode over the rocks, sniffing here and turning a rock over there, pausing now and then to lift his leg.

"What do you think he is after?" I asked Roger.

"Foxes, I expect. It is just the time of year that the vixen takes the cubs out for the first time."

The wolf looked magnificent, primeval and majestic. He sauntered fearlessly past, giving us one scathing look.

A snowy owl flew down quite near and looked at us too, then lifted its shoulders, spread its gigantic wings and followed the wolf down towards the river.

The sun was clear now, no mist veiling it from our sight.

"Look at it," said Roger. "It's nearly down behind that hill. Once it goes completely behind that shoulder it won't come back again until next February."

"Come on," said Hugh. "Time to go for us too."

I stood for a while, breathing the crisp air. Physically, I felt a complete and entire renovation of my body. I knew that every muscle was in tune and could rise to any occasion asked of it. Intellectually and morally, the continual struggle had made me more energetic and self-reliant, more calm and tranquil, steady in presence of danger, level-headed in judging a difficulty, cool, resolute and firm in solving it. The mental strain of the last nine months had the effect of mental gymnastics. I was "exercised" in quick assessments, rapid decisions, the perception and analysis of a situation. My temperament was more gentle, less exacting and more tolerant than when we arrived in the north. Bertrand Russell said that "life is all a matter of priorities", and I felt that I had sorted mine out. I was thin and strong, hardened and inured to every sort of fatigue, I could easily cope with life in the north, but—how about civilisation? I needed friends, and my family, also a community to belong to.

The sky was a pale blue, the sea gently white, and the land russet and brown. The mountains of Ellesmere Island were still a hard line against the filmy horizon, across the Sound. A restless breeze rustled my long hair, whipping the tears of emotion out of my eyes. I started to run after the others, following the gorge of the river. It swept relentlessly along below me; I could sense the force of it grinding into the walls of rock that hemmed it in. A neat little fox suddenly stood up in my path, trotted off, then crouched down and mewed at me like an alley-cat tom. I resisted the urge to look for her cubs. No time left. I ran on, into the now rising sun. The rocks were dry, and there was a sensuous satisfaction in jumping from one to the other, one's feet perfectly balanced for an instant's contact with the rock.

The river fell into the sea at an arm at the head of the bay. The water exploded out of the confining walls of the gorge, roaring with relief, and dropped into the sea, which hardly rippled. A tern was plunging down into the water, uttering a harsh "kree-e". A slim and graceful long-tailed skua was fishing for itself alongside. It was probably preparing for its long migration across vast distances of sea without food. The long-tailed skua wander far and wide. I had seen one when crossing the ice-cap of Greenland, where it was hundreds of miles from its food, and Freuchen met them on every excursion into the interior of north-east Greenland. Sitting a little farther out in the bay, on a grounded iceberg, was a medium-sized gull, pure white, with a yellowish bill and black feet. It was an Ivory gull, the true bird of the Polar sea. It spends the whole year in the fields of pack and drifting ice, only resorting to land to breed. Even then it chooses a place of snow and ice, and nests on the coast of Spitzbergen and Franz Joseph Land, in a cold inaccessible spot. This one now flew towards me, like a pigeon in a park, and alighted to see if I had anything dead for it to eat. It looked at me disdainfully, and went off to search for a polar bear who might have left it some offal from a seal.

Hugh and Roger were striding away across the tundra, and I ran to catch them up. We crept past the silent huts, and down to our tent. I kicked off my boots and inched into the sleeping-bag between Rona and Rory. I was tired after our fifteen-mile walk.

"Oh, good," said Rona, sitting up. "It's breakfast time." Hugh was still snoring. But there was no let up for me! Robin and Bruce were wild with excitement. "It's clear," they shouted. "The plane will come. Home today."

"I'm going to ring Malcolm's door and get him out for a game of footie," said Robin with conviction, as if we were there already. Distance has no place in a child's mind.

We leant over the sleeping Hugh, stood on him and spilt water over him as I set about finding breakfast. I was stirring our porridge in the blackened billy-can when suddenly a roar outdid the noise of the Primus.

"The plane. The plane," shrieked the children, throwing the tent into confusion. The sound was intolerable, then it toned down into that of fifty Hoovers. Still Hugh slept! The plane turned, now on the ground, and taxied towards us. A mini-blizzard hit the tent, and it collapsed in a muddle of canvas. The pilot stepped down. "Ready?" he enquired. "Must get out before the fog comes in again."

Bemused, Hugh appeared, feet first. "How about some coffee?" he asked the pilot, hospitably, ignoring the fact that our camp was in chaos.

"No time," answered the pilot. The hut door now opened, and the scientists, looking organised and fed, strolled down towards the runway.

"Quick. Quick," urged the pilot, on the hop, and the men from the huts enthusiastically helped us depart. They passed up armfuls of unpacked sleeping-bag and packets of oats, loose dirty nappies and Bruce's whalebones. There was no time to be sentimental. Suddenly we had left our glen. The plane banked against the buttress of rock limiting the ice-cap, and turned away from Devon Island, out over the sea. The North-West Passage was below us, and I felt that the wheel had turned a full cycle. Frobisher, Davies, Hudson, Parry, Franklin and M'Clintock had their lives tied to that ribbon of water that wound between the ice beneath our little plane. It all looked so easy. And now all those efforts had been justified—the North-West Passage was important again. Oil must be transported south to the hungry, greedy motors that civilisation is totally dependent upon. A vast tanker was at that minute thrusting its way between Baffin and Devon Islands, heading for Resolute. Lady Franklin would have been pleased . . . her husband had shown the way. But I was not. No benefits would be reaped in the Eskimo settlements, but the total death-knell to their way of life. Why, oh why, did we presume that our way must be best? What "culture" was being offered to replace that being swept away by the riff-raff of oil-thirsty Americans and Canadians, who should have known better than rape their own land? They were only interested in what could be "got". No one was "giving" any more.

My thoughts turned again to Lady Franklin. She was the

only woman to be involved with the Arctic for as long as I.
She would be the only person to whom I would not have to
explain why I needed to come back.

I looked around at my family, unwashed and unkempt. The
children's bright eyes shone out of their ruddy, animated faces.
Their minds had not been blunted by the months of hard living.
They had to go home for an education, but where would I find
one for them that would teach them that the amassing of
knowledge was incidental, and that the important fact of life
was the ability to work; to apply one's mind to solve a difficulty
for oneself, and that there is no jungle so against one as the urban,
overpopulated, civilised one we live in today. To be able to
cope, one must be mentally and morally strong, to a level never
necessary before.

Our belongings were in confusion. "Never mind," I thought,
"we will spend three or four days in Resolute, getting organised:
hot baths; the huge washing machine belonging to the met.
boys; the shop selling toothpaste and shampoo; the library;
the bar! the food!"

"There's the end of Devon," shouted Robin, craning his
neck to look back. A steep escarpment fell into the greyish-
white, waterlogged ice, that signified the sea between Cornwallis
Island and Devon.

"That's where we finished our journey," said Roger, "when
Wally and I came from Greenland, last year."

"It's the end of ours, too," said Bruce mournfully, then
added, "What about pocket money when we get home, Mum?
You must owe us thousands of pounds."

It was a different Resolute that we flew into that autumn day
from when we had arrived the previous January.

"Hello," said the airport manager, our friend, George Jost.
"You are just in time for the Montreal plane. I am holding it
for you here on the runway."

Our unpacked belongings were carried by many hands
straight from Weldy's little place across to the big jet.

"But, but . . ." I said. "I haven't packed yet and I'm still
in my filthy jeans."

"Have to do it in Montreal," said Roger. "We can't not
get on the plane when he has kept it waiting."

Hostile eyes looked us up and down as we climbed in, like a party of gypsies. Well-dressed women turned aside and the men looked even more disdainful. There was a party of Eskimo children in front of the plane and thankfully I sat down among them, feeling more at home.

"When do we get some food?" asked the children excitedly. I looked at their black ingrained nails and wondered if the trim air hostess would consider serving them anything!

We reached Montreal at 1 a.m.

"Oh," I said to Hugh. "Just book us in at the most expensive hotel, for three days, till we get organised. A really good one with plenty of baths and swimming pools and lashings of good food."

Hugh left me to go ahead to the centre of the air terminal. He rushed back a few minutes later.

"Quick, quick," he said. "They are pushing us on a BOAC plane this minute."

"What?" I said, aghast, looking at what I clutched in my hand; it was the blackened billy-can of this morning's porridge.

I handed it to Robin. "Get rid of this quick," I said, "for heaven's sake."

"Where?" he asked, looking around uselessly.

"I don't care. Just lose it."

Officials bundled us on again and in no time at all we were collapsing in the plush seats of the transatlantic plane.

"Oh," said an air hostess turning up her nose. "You left this behind." She handed me the blackened billy-can!

Our minds numbed, we droned across the Atlantic. The green of the old world enveloped us at Shannon.

"Look, look," said the children, breathless with excitement. "Look at that grass."

"Oh," said Rona. "You haven't got any of those flowers in your press. Shall I get out and pick some? Buttercups! Look there's a cow!"

The passengers looked round and giggled at her naïveté.

"You know," said the air hostess helpfully. "They sell baby clothes in the shop at the airport terminal."

I realised that Rory was the scruffiest of the lot. He had outgrown his clothes by several inches. I did not dare refuse the hint of the hostess and shamefacedly crept out of the plane, clutching a wriggling Rory. I plonked him down on the counter and a kindly Irish girl rushed to oblige.

"Here's a genuine linen suit, hand-stitched and embroidered in Donegal. It only costs £5."

"Hurry," said the air hostess who had followed me down. "Yes, he'll look delightful in that. Do let me put it on."

I longed for the Arctic where decisions were my own. Here already other people were making them for me. Clad in his new clothes Rory was handed from air hostess to air hostess. In his old clothes he had been shunned by the lot.

We tumbled out at Prestwick, vacant with sleeplessness and churned-up rhythms. Clutching armfuls of baggage still unpacked we staggered towards the barrier. A customs man was waving his arms in horror in our direction.

"Oh," said Robin. "I think he wants the billy-can."

I handed it to him, thankfully.

"I only require the contents, Madam," he said. "I will return the container if you fill in this form. We're used to everything here," he said cheerfully. "Pakistanis with cardboard bundles, Jamaicans with home brews and er . . . doctors with billy-cans of porridge. Now what did you say was in all these samples?"

"Urine," said Hugh in a loud clear voice.

"What did you say?" said the customs man.

"Urine," chimed in all the children. "You must have heard of that."

APPENDIX I

APPENDIX I

Decrement of Strength in Hand Grip during a Static Simulation
(living a 21-hour day) of an Eastbound Circumglobal Flight

21-hour days	Degrees longitude covered	Grip-strength in pounds	Probability of difference
	say		
1.	0–45 (Greenwich to Moscow)	99	
2.	45–90 (Baghdad to Calcutta)	97	
3.	90–135 (Rangoon to Tokyo)	93	Mean of days
4.	135–180 (Kamchatka to Aleutians)	91	1, 2, 7, 8 and
5.	180–225 (Bering Straits to Alaska)	90	days 3, 4, 5, 6
6.	225–270 (Alaska to Denver)	96	by 't' test
7.	270–315 (Minneapolis to New-foundland)	96	$P \equiv \cdot 001$
8.	315–360 (Greenland to Green-wich)	99	

(Pooled results of R.T. and H.S. over three weeks living on a 21-hour day
based on 187 observations in Devon Island using a hydraulic dynamometer)

APPENDIX II

(detailed by Roger Tufft)

APPENDIX II

Sledge Loading

Non-Consumable	lb.
Sledge, complete	53
Sleeping bag, three man	14
Tent, three man	25
Cooking utensils	8
Rifle	6
Pack frames, three	7
Skis and sticks	30
Spare runners, two	24
Ice axes, two	4
Radio	39
Generator	47
Sextant, R.D.F., cameras	48
Medical Research	19
Personal bags, including repair kit and ammunition	26
	350

Consumable	
Food, three "sixty man days"	440
Paraffin, 10 gallons	95
Petrol, 2 gallons	17
	552

Total 902 lb.

Log

All times are local—G.M.T.—6 hrs.

February	Hours Travelled	Remarks	Distance
21	1400–1530	Relaying Ice Shelf	¾ m.
22	1310–1500	Relaying	1 m.
23	1100–2100	Relaying	3 m.
24	1200–1500	Back Packing. On to Sea Ice	200 yards
25	1000–1500	Triple Relay	1 m.
26	0950–1730	Triple and Half relays	1 m.
27	0830–1500	Triple and Double relays	½ m.
28	1000–1600	Double relay	1 m.
March 1	1010–1600	⅓ and ½ loads. Two-hour break 21 m.	1 m.
2	1015–1600	⅓ and ½ loads	¾ m.
3	1215–1545	½ loads	1 m.
4	0930–1700	½ loads	3 m.
5	0930–1700	½ loads. Sun appeared	2 m.
6	0930–1300	½ loads	1½ m.
7	0900–1600	½ loads	3 m.
8	1200–1700	½ loads	2 m.
9	0930–1635	Single load and ½ load	2½ m.
10	1520–1700	1 load. Throwaway camp	2 m.
11	0920–1700	1 load and ½ load	6 m.
12	1400–1705	1 load	3 m.
13	0900–1640	1 load	6 m.
14	1200–1645	1 load	4 m.
15		No move. "Fall in" camp	0 m.
16	0830–1630	1 load	8 m.
17	0840–1620	1 load	6 m.
18	0850–1640	1 load	6 m.
19	1300–1730	1 load	3 m.
20	0800–1330	1 load	3 m.
21	0820–1430	1 load	5 m.
22	0800–1715	1 load (two-hour break)	4 m.
23	0915–1600	1 load	5 m.
24	0800–1630	1 load	6 m.
25	0830–1545	1 load and back packing	4 m.
26		Return camp at La84°42° by sextant	0 m.
			96 m.

March	Hours Travelled	Remarks	Distance
27	0930–1820	1 load ⎤	13 m.
28	0820–1710		10 m.
29	0810–1800	(two and half hour break)	11 m.
30	0730–1530		11 m.
31	0730–1720		10 m.
April 1	0730–1930	(two and a quarter hour break	9 m.
2	0900–1745	(two hour break)	9 m.
3	0850–1930		13 m.
4	0945–1845		8 m.
5	Open water. Lie up		0 m.
6	0515–1230	Reached land after 1 mile on ice ⎦	5 m.
			—
			99 m.
			—

Returned to Ward Hunt after 45 days
February–April 1969

Synopsis of Meteorological Observations

NOTES

1. Instruments — Two standard U.S. meteorological thermometers were used. The ordinary thermometer was exposed some minutes prior to observations. As far as possible it was kept out of wind and direct sunlight. The minimum thermometer was exposed overnight as far as possible in a sheltered position on the sledge, some two to three feet above the ground.

2. Observations — Observations were normally made at 0900, 1200, 1500, 1900 local time (i.e. G.M.T. minus 6 hours). On days when only three observations are recorded, the 1800 observation was missed.

3. The Tables

All temperatures are MINUS in degrees Fahrenheit.

(a) Daily temperatures are the average of 3 or 4 readings.
(b) The minimum temperature is the minimum temperature of the previous night.
(c) Snow and drift refer to conditions at the time of the various observations.
(d) Visibility is ESTIMATED IN MILES
(e) Cloud cover is ESTIMATED IN OKTAS (eighths)

(*f*) Wind speed is ESTIMATED IN KNOTS
(*g*) Wind direction is ESTIMATED
    N = between NW and NE
    S = between SW and SE
    E = between NE and SE
    W = between SW and NW

FEBRUARY

Day	No. of Obs.	Minus °F Temperature Av. Temp.	Night Min.	Precipitation Snow	Drift	Visibility <1	1-10	10-20	>20	Cloud 0	1-4	4-8	Fog	Wind Speed Calm	0-5	5-10	10-20	Wind Direction N	S	E	W
23	3	33·5	38				2		1	1	1	1		3							
24	3	39·0	36						3	1	3			3	1					1	
25	3	31·0	51						3	3				2	1				1		
26	3	35·0	41				2	3				3		2							
27	2	30·0	38					3			3	2		2							
28	3	49·0	50					3				2		3							
Total	17			0	0		4	6	7	4	4	9	0	14	2	0	0	0	1	1	0
Av.		36·0	42·5																		

MARCH

Day	No. of Obs.	Minus °F Temperature Av. Temp.	Night Min.	Precipitation Snow	Drift	Visibility <1	1-10	10-20	>20	Cloud 0	1-4	4-8	Fog	Wind Speed Calm	0-5	5-10	10-20	Wind Direction N	S	E	W
1	3	51·5	54						3		3			2	1					1	
2	3	54·5	56	2					3		3			3							
3	3	54·5	59				2	2	1		1	2		2	1						
4	3	49·5	49		4			1	1		3					2				1	
5	3	44·5	46		3		2				3		2			3	1			3	
6	3	41·5	44		2		3				3						3			3	
7	3	42·0	43		3	3				3							3			3	
8	3	40·4	38			3	2			3						1	2			2	
9	3	36·5	39				3		1		1						3				
10	3	38·5	50							2	3			3							
11	4	46·5	49	2	3				3		4	3			3		1			1	
12	4	39·0	39				2	2	4		2	1		1		2					3
13	4	39·5	58		3	3	4		2	1		4		4	3						
14	4	44·0	49	2			1		2		1	4		1			4				4
15	4	40·0	38	3			1	3				3				1					2
16	4	33·0	32				4				1	3		2	1						2
17	4	34·0	43	2				3				4	1	2	3						2
18	4	30·0	36			1			4	1	2	2		2	2						1
19	4	34·0	44					3			3					1	2			2	1
20	3	40·0	46						4	1		3		1	2						2
21	4	37·5	51							4	1	4	1	3							1
22	4	32·0	44	1	1		4			2				1	1	1	1				1
23	4	39·0	28	3	2	4			3	2	1	4		1		1	3				2
24	4	23·5	28			1	1		3	2	1			3	1					1	1

Day	No. of Obs.	Av. Temp.	Night Min.	Snow	Drift	<1	1–10	10–20	>20	0	1–4	4–8	Fog	Calm	0–5	5–10	10–20	N	S	E	W
25	4	27·0	36		2			3											2		3
26	4	33·0	40																	4	
27	4	35·5	35									3			1	4				4	4
28	4	34·5	42			1	1		3	1	1	3		2	4	1				2	2
29	4	38·0	44			1	1	3	3	2	2	2			2						
30	4	31·5	44					3	4	4	4			4		1	3				
31	4	20·9	29					4						4							4
Total	**113**	Av. 37·5	43·0	14	20	11	34	25	43	27	42	43	3	38	33	11	28	0	0	31	26

APRIL

		Minus °F Temperature		Precipitation		Visibility				Cloud				Wind Speed				Wind Direction			
Day	No. of Obs.	Av. Temp.	Night Min.	Snow	Drift	<1	1–10	10–20	>20	0	1–4	4–8	Fog	Calm	0–5	5–10	10–20	N	S	E	W
1	4	29·5	34		3		1	3			4			1			3				
2	4	26·0	34						4	4					4				2		
3	4	21·5	32		4	4				4					4						4
4	4	15·0	32					4			4			2	2						
5	4	6·5	21						4	2	2						4				4
6	4	5·5	12					4				4		4							
7	4	15·5	21				1	3				4		4							
Total	**28**	Av. 17·0	26·5	0	7	4	2	14	8	10	10	8	0	11	10	0	7	0	2	0	8

INDEX

INDEX